ROYAL COURT

Royal Court Theatre presents

THE PEOPLE ARE FRIENDLY

by **Michael Wynne**

First performance at the Royal Court Jerwood Theatre Downstairs
Sloane Square, London on 7 June 2002.

Supported by Jerwood New P

JERWOOD
NEW PL

THE PEOPLE ARE FRIENDLY

by **Michael Wynne**

Cast in order of appearance
Robert Williamson **Stephen Mangan**
Michelle Hanlon **Sally Rogers**
Kathleen Hanlon **Sue Jenkins**
Donna Hanlon **Michelle Butterly**
Brian Yates **Nick Moss**
John Hanlon **Alan Williams**
Kirsty Hanlon **Sheridan Smith**
Eddie Yates **Joe Cooper, Jack Richards**

Director **Dominic Cooke**
Designer **John Stevenson**
Lighting Designer **Peter Mumford**
Sound Designer **Paul Arditti**
Assistant Director **Jo Combes**
Casting Director **Lisa Makin**
Production Manager **Paul Handley**
Company Stage Manager **Cath Binks**
Stage Manager **Suzanne Bourke**
Deputy Stage Manger **Dani Youngman**
Assistant Stage Manager **Nicole Keighley**
Costume Supervisor **Iona Kenrick**
Wardrobe Mistress **Jackie Orton**
Fight Coach **Terry King**
Dialect Coach **Penny Dyer**
Company Voice Work **Patsy Rodenburg**
Set Built By **Rupert Blakeley**

Royal Court Theatre would like to thank the following for their help with this production:
Wardrobe care by Persil and Comfort courtesy of Lever Fabergé.

THE COMPANY

Michael Wynne (writer)
For the Royal Court: The Knocky.
Other theatre includes: Sell Out (Frantic Assembly),
The Boy Who Left Home (Actors Touring
Company), Too Cold For Snow (Prada Foundation).
Awards include: The Meyer Whitworth Award,
Liverpool Echo Arts Awards Best New Talent for
The Knocky and Time Out Best Off-West End
Production Award for Sell Out.

Paul Arditti (sound designer)
Paul Arditti has been designing sound for theatre
since 1983, including over 70 shows for the Royal
Court.
Productions for the Royal Court include: Where Do
We Live, The Night Heron, Plasticine, Boy Gets
Girl, Clubland, Blasted, Mouth To Mouth, Spinning
Into Butter, I Just Stopped By To See The Man, Far
Away, My Zinc Bed, 4.48 Psychosis, Fireface, Mr
Kolpert, The Force of Change, Other People,
Dublin Carol, The Glory of Living, The Kitchen, Rat
in the Skull, Some Voices, Mojo, The Weir; The
Steward of Christendom, Shopping and Fucking,
Blue Heart (co-productions with Out of Joint); The
Chairs (co-production with Theatre de Complicite);
Cleansed, Via Dolorosa.
Other theatre includes: Hinterland (Out of Joint);
Afore Night Come (Young Vic); Tales From
Hollywood (Donmar); Light (Complicite); Our Lady
of Sligo (RNT with Out of Joint); Some Explicit
Polaroids (Out of Joint); Hamlet, The Tempest
(RSC); Orpheus Descending, Cyrano de Bergerac,
St Joan (West End); Marathon (Gate).
Musicals include: Doctor Dolittle, Piaf, The
Threepenny Opera.
Awards include: Drama Desk Award for
Outstanding Sound Design 1992 for Four Baboons
Adoring the Sun (Broadway).

Michelle Butterly
Theatre includes: Safe (Carob Theatre/TIE tour);
Road, Shakers (Wolsey Theatre, Ipswich); Peggy
Buck, Lent (Belgrade); The Party's Over (Playhouse,
Nottingham); End of the Food Chain (Stephen
Joseph Theatre, Scarborough); Laundry Room at
the Hotel Madrid (Gate); Gaslight (Theatr Clwyd);
The Servant to Two Masters (RSC/Young Vic/USA/
Albery/tour).
Television includes: Dangerfield, Pie in The Sky,
Hetty Wainthrop Investigates, Soldier, Soldier (one
series), St Clare, The Echo, Heartbeat, Casualty
(two series).

Jo Combes (assistant director)
As assistant director, theatre includes: Picasso's
Women (national tour); West Side Story
(Greenwich); Clockwatching, Wild, Wild
Women, The Captain's Tiger (Orange Tree).
As director, theatre includes: Women of Troy,
Macbeth (Orange Tree); Drawn from Life
(Bare Boards at the Finborough); The Tempest
(Southwark Playhouse).
Jo's work on this production is supported by
the Channel Four/ Royal Court Theatre Drama
Directors Programme.

Dominic Cooke (director)
Associate Director of the Royal Court.
For the Royal Court: Plasticine, Fucking
Games, Redundant, Spinning into Butter,
Fireface, Other People.
Other theatre includes: As adapter and
director: Arabian Nights (Young Vic/UK and
world tour/ New Victory Theatre, New York).
As director: Hunting Scenes From Lower
Bavaria, The Weavers (Gate), Afore Night
Come, Entertaining Mr Sloane (Theatr Clwyd);
The Bullet (Donmar Warehouse); My Mother
Said I Never Should (Oxford Stage Company/
Young Vic); Of Mice and Men (Nottingham
Playhouse); Kiss Of the Spiderwoman (Bolton
Octagon); Autogeddon (Edinburgh Assembly
Rooms); Caravan (National Theatre of
Norway); The Importance of Being Earnest
(Atlantic Theatre Festival, Canada).
Opera includes: I Capuleti e i Montacchi
(Grange Park Opera).
Awards include: TMA Award for Arabian
Nights, Manchester Evening News Drama
Award for The Marriage of Figaro and
Edinburgh Fringe First for Autogeddon.
Assistant Director at the Royal Shakespeare
Company 1992-94.

Joe Cooper
The People Are Friendly is Joe's first
professional production.

Sue Jenkins

Theatre includes: Tom Jones, The Devils, School For Wives, Sisterly Feelings, Educating Rita, Golden Girls (Leeds Playhouse); Having a Ball, Breezeblock Park (Theatre Royal, York); Good Witness for the Prosecution, Educating Rita (Harrogate); The Collector, The Party's Over, The Rocky Horror Show, Tommy, It's a Madhouse (Coliseum Theatre, Oldham); Twelfth Night, Othello, As You Like It, The Servant of Two Masters, Enemy of the People, The Winslow Boy, Absurd Person Singular, Absent Friends (Octagon, Bolton); The Changeling, The Plough and the Stars, Savage Amusement, The Ragged Trousered Philanthropist (Contact); While The Sun Shines (Liverpool Playhouse).

Television includes: Merseybeat, In Deep, Brookside (11 years), In Suspicious Circumstances, Coasting, Coronation Street (four years), The Beiderbecke Affair, How We Used To Live.

Radio includes: Wuthering Heights, Middlemarch, Villette, The Jew of Malta.

Stephen Mangan

Theatre includes: Noises Off (Piccadilly Theatre); Hay Fever (Savoy); Much Ado About Nothing (Cheek by Jowl); She Stoops To Conquer (Birmingham Stage Co); A Midsummer Night's Dream, School for Scandal (RSC); As You Like It, Twelfth Night, The Tempest (Nottingham Playhouse); Hamlet (Theatre Royal, Norwich); Couch Grass & Ribbon (Watermill, Newbury); The Rover (Salisbury Playhouse); The Tempest (Nottingham Playhouse & Theatr Clwyd); The Shoe Shop of Desire (Nottingham Playhouse & RNT); George Dandin, Mrs Warren's Profession (Redgrave).

Television includes: I'm Still Alan Partridge, Lucky Jim, The Cappuccino Years, Sword of Honour, The Armando Ianucchi Shows, Human Remains, In Defence, Big Bad World, Watership Down.

Film includes: Birthday Girl, Chunky Monkey, Martha Meets..., Billy Elliot.

Radio includes: The Man Who Knew Everything, Into Exile, A Midsummer Nights Dream, As You Like It.

Nick Moss

For the Royal Court: Made of Stone (Exposure, Royal Court Young Writers Festival).

Other theatre includes: Enjoy (West Yorkshire Playhouse); An Evening With Gary Lineker (Oldham Coliseum); The Snow Queen (Library Theatre Co, Manchester); A Man From The Motor Show (I.L.T); Having a Ball, Man of the Moment (Theatre Royal, York); End of Season (Canada Theatre Direct); Scouse (Everyman, Liverpool); W.A.T.E.R is Water (Theatr Clywd); Bonded (Sheffield Crucible); Strippers (Oldham Coliseum); End of Season (Red Ladder).

Television includes: Paradise Heights, Smack the Pony, Mersey Beat, Casualty, Doctors, Always & Everyone, Liverpool One, Lifeforce, Heartbeat, City Central, The Cops, Retrace, Hillsborough, Police 2020, Emmerdale.

Film includes: Mean Machine, Al's Lads, Going Off Big Time, Heart.

Radio includes: Chaos by Design, Absolute Beginners.

Peter Mumford (lighting designer)

For the Royal Court: Redundant.

Other theatre includes: Private Lives (Albery & Broadway); The Feast of Snails (Lyric); Luther, Bacchae, Van Gogh in Brixton, House of Secrets, Summerfolk, The Merchant of Venice, Money, The Prime of Miss Jean Brodie (RNT); Hamlet, Othello, The Taming of the Shrew (RSC); Iphigenia (Abbey, Dublin); God Only Knows (Vaudeville); Medea (Queen's); The Dispute & The Critic (Royal Exchange, Manchester); Lautrec (Shaftesbury); A Long Day's Journey into Night, An Ideal Husband, Oliver Twist, Therese Raquin (Gate, Dublin).

Opera includes: I Laskarina (Acropol Theatre, Athens); The Bartered Bride (ROH); Earth and the Great Weather (also directed, Almeida Opera 2000); Un Ballo In Maschera (Vilinius Festival); Don Pasquale (Opera Zuid, Holland); The Coronation of Poppaea (ENO); Eugene Onegin, Madame Butterfly (Opera North); Guilio Cesare (Opera de Bordeaux).

Dance includes: A Stranger's Taste, This House Will Burn (Royal Ballet); Of Oil and Water (Siobhan Davies Dance Co.); Irek Mukhamedov and Dancers (Sadler's Wells); Arthur (Birmingham Royal Ballet); The Crucible, Hidden Variables, A Stranger's Taste, This House Will Burn (Royal Ballet); Sounding, Unrest, The Celebrated Soubrette (Rambert Dance Co.). Peter won the Laurence Olivier Award for Outstanding Achievement in Dance for The Glass Blew In and Fearful Symmetries and was nominated for Best Lighting Designer in 2000.

Jack Richards

Theatre includes: Medea (Queens).

Television includes: Daylight Robbery (2 series), Trombone.

Film includes: Mothertime (National Film School).

Sally Rogers

For the Royal Court: Killing the Cat, Uganda; Blue Heart (co-production with Out of Joint). Other theatre includes: Black Snow, Arturo Ui, Murmuring Judges, Billy Liar (RNT); A Midsummer Night's Dream (Chester Gateway); Blithe Spirit (Bristol Old Vic); Our Country's Good, Some Explicit Polaroids, Rita, Sue and Bob Too, A State Affair (Out of Joint).
Television includes: Eastenders, 3 Fights, 2 Weddings and a Funeral, Paul Calf's Video Diary, Get Calf, Seaforth, Dangerfield, A Touch of Frost, London Bridge, Beyond Fear, Casualty, The Lakes, Out of Hours, Playing the Field III, Attachments, Murphy's Law.
Film includes: A Short History of Ten Pin Bowling, A Demon in My View, Top Dog.

Sheridan Smith

Theatre includes: Ancient Lights (Hampstead); Into the Woods (Donmar); Tin Pan Ali, She Stoops To Conquer (NYMT); Bugsy Malone (Queens); The Wizard of Oz (Plowright, Scunthorpe); Pendragon (NYMT/New York); Annie (Hull New Theatre/Doncaster Civic/ Crucible, Sheffield).
Television includes: Two Pints of Lager and a Packet of Crisps (three series), Whitby Royal, Fat Friends, Blood Strangers, Always and Everyone, Holby City, The Royle Family (two series), Where The Heart Is, Hawkins, Doctors, Going Out, Heartbeat, Anchor Me, The Strangerers, Dark Ages, Wives and Daughters.
Film includes: Peaches.

John Stevenson (designer)

For the Royal Court: Spinning Into Butter. Other theatre includes: Penelope (Guildhall School of Music and Drama); Wuthering Heights, Coriolanus (West Yorkshire Playhouse); Ubu Kunst (Young Vic/Bobigney Paris); Get Back in the Box (Round House Camden); Farndale Mysteries (Brewhouse Theatre Taunton); Someone Who'll Watch Over Me (Theatr Clwyd); The Shoe Horn Sonata (Kings Head); Albertine in Five Times (The Bridewell).
Dance includes: Cinderella (City Ballet of London).
Television includes: Manchild, Estate Agents.
Film includes: Taking the Light (Third Man Films), Tomorrow La Scala (BBC Films/Home Movies), Young Offenders (BBC Films).

Alan Williams

For the Royal Court: Crave (touring production produced by Paines Plough and Bright Ltd), Local, Bed of Roses, Weekend After Next (also Hull Truck tour).
Other theatre includes: The Inland Sea (Oxford Stage Co); The Sea (Chichester Festival); Casanova (tour); The Jew of Malta (Almeida and tour); The Rib Cage, To the Chicago Abyss (Royal Exchange); Kiss the Sky (Bush); Vigil (Arts Club Theatre, Vancouver); The Darling Family (Theatre Passe Muraille, Toronto); White Dogs of Texas (Tarragon Theatre, Toronto and tour); The Cockroach Trilogy (Hull Truck tour UK/US/ Canada); Having a Ball (Liverpool Playhouse); Mean Streaks (also Bush), Bed of Roses (Hull Truck tour); Small Ads (King's Head); Mary Barnes (Birmingham Rep); Prejudice, Eejits (Liverpool Everyman).
Television includes: Paradise Heights, Wire in the Blood, Sirens, Peak Practice, The Mayor of Casterbridge, Love in a Cold Climate, Badger, Coronation Street, Always & Everyone, The Bill, Touching Evil, Getting Hurt, The Scold's Bridle, Wycliffe.
Film includes: Heartlands, All Or Nothing, Unconditional Love, Elephant Juice, Among Giants, The Cockroach That Ate Cincinatti, Coleslaw Warehouse, The Darling Family, Daughters of the Country.

THE ENGLISH STAGE COMPANY AT THE ROYAL COURT

The English Stage Company at the Royal Court opened in 1956 as a subsidised theatre producing new British plays, international plays and some classical revivals.

The first artistic director George Devine aimed to create a writers' theatre, 'a place where the dramatist is acknowledged as the fundamental creative force in the theatre and where the play is more important than the actors, the director, the designer'. The urgent need was to find a contemporary style in which the play, the acting, direction and design are all combined. He believed that 'the battle will be a long one to continue to create the right conditions for writers to work in'.

Devine aimed to discover 'hard-hitting, uncompromising writers whose plays are stimulating, provocative and exciting'. The Royal Court production of John Osborne's Look Back in Anger in May 1956 is now seen as the decisive starting point of modern British drama and the policy created a new generation of British playwrights. The first wave included John Osborne, Arnold Wesker, John Arden, Ann Jellicoe, N F Simpson and Edward Bond. Early seasons included new international plays by Bertolt Brecht, Eugène Ionesco, Samuel Beckett, Jean-Paul Sartre and Marguerite Duras.

The theatre started with the 400-seat proscenium arch Theatre Downstairs, and then in 1969 opened a second theatre, the 60-seat studio Theatre Upstairs. Some productions transfer to the West End, such as Caryl Churchill's Far Away, Conor McPherson's The Weir, Kevin Elyot's Mouth to Mouth and My Night With Reg. The Royal Court also co-produces plays which have transferred to the West End or toured internationally, such as Sebastian Barry's The Steward of Christendom and Mark Ravenhill's Shopping and Fucking (with Out of Joint), Martin McDonagh's The Beauty Queen Of Leenane (with Druid Theatre Company), Ayub Khan-Din's East is East (with Tamasha Theatre Company, and now a feature film).

Since 1994 the Royal Court's artistic policy has again been vigorously directed to finding and producing a new generation of playwrights. The writers include Joe Penhall, Rebecca Prichard, Michael Wynne, Nick Grosso, Judy Upton, Meredith Oakes, Sarah Kane, Anthony Neilson, Judith Johnson, James Stock, Jez Butterworth, Marina Carr, Simon Block, Martin McDonagh, Mark Ravenhill, Ayub Khan-Din, Tamantha Hammerschlag, Jess Walters, Che Walker, Conor McPherson, Simon Stephens, Richard Bean, Roy

photo: Andy Chopping

Williams, Gary Mitchell, Mick Mahoney, Rebecca Gilman, Christopher Shinn, Kia Corthron, David Gieselmann, Marius von Mayenburg, David Eldridge, Leo Butler, Zinnie Harris, Grae Cleugh, Roland Schimmelpfennig and Vassily Sigarev. This expanded programme of new plays has been made possible through the support of A.S.K Theater Projects, the Jerwood Charitable Foundation, the American Friends of the Royal Court Theatre and many in association with the Royal National Theatre Studio.

In recent years there have been record-breaking productions at the box office, with capacity houses for Rebecca Gilman's Boy Gets Girl, Kevin Elyot's Mouth To Mouth, David Hare's My Zinc Bed and Conor McPherson's The Weir, which transferred to the West End in October 1998 and ran for nearly two years at the Duke of York's Theatre.

The newly refurbished theatre in Sloane Square opened in February 2000, with a policy still inspired by the first artistic director George Devine. The Royal Court is an international theatre for new plays and new playwrights, and the work shapes contemporary drama in Britain and overseas.

REBUILDING THE ROYAL COURT

In 1995, the Royal Court was awarded a National Lottery grant through the Arts Council of England, to pay for three quarters of a £26m project to completely rebuild its 100-year old home. The rules of the award required the Royal Court to raise £7.6m in partnership funding. The building has been completed thanks to the generous support of those listed below.

We are particularly grateful for the contributions of over 5,700 audience members.

English Stage Company Registered Charity number 231242.

THE AMERICAN FRIENDS OF THE ROYAL COURT THEATRE

AFRCT support the mission of the Royal Court and are primarily focused on raising funds to enable the theatre to produce new work by emerging American writers. Since this not-for-profit organisation was founded in 1997, AFRCT has contributed to eight productions including Christopher Shinn's Where Do We Live. They have also supported the participation of young artists in the Royal Court's acclaimed International Residency.

If you would like to support the ongoing work of the Royal Court, please contact the Development Department on 020 7565 5050.

ROYAL COURT
DEVELOPMENT BOARD
Tamara Ingram (Chair)
Jonathan Cameron
(Vice Chair)
Timothy Burrill
Anthony Burton
Jonathan Caplan QC
Deborah Davis
Cecily Engle
Kimberly Fortier
Julia Hobsbawm
Joyce Hytner
Mary Ellen Johnson
Dan Klein
Michael Potter
Mark Robinson
William Russell
Sue Stapely
James L Tanner
Will Turner

PRINCIPAL DONOR
Jerwood Foundation

WRITERS CIRCLE
The Cadogan Estate
Carillon/Schal
News International plc
Pathé
The Eva and Hans K
Rausing Trust
The Rayne Foundation
Sky
Garfield Weston
Foundation

DIRECTORS CIRCLE
The Esmée Fairbairn
Foundation
The Granada Group plc

ACTORS CIRCLE
Edwin C Cohen & The
Blessing Way Foundation
Sir Ronald Cohen &
Sharon Harel-Cohen
Quercus Charitable Trust
The Basil Samuel
Charitable Trust

The Trusthouse
Charitable Foundation
The Woodward
Charitable Trust

SPECIFIC DONATIONS
The Foundation for
Sport and the Arts for
Stage System
John Lewis Partnership
plc for Balcony
City Parochial
Foundation for Infra
Red Induction Loops
and Toilets for Disabled
Patrons
RSA Art for
Architecture Award
Scheme for Antoni
Malinowski Wall
Painting

AMERICAN FRIENDS

Founders
Harry Brown and Richard
Walsh
Francis Finlay
Amanda Foreman and
Jonathan Barton
Monica Gerard-Sharp and
Ali Wambold
Jeananne Hauswald
Mary Ellen Johnson and
Richard Goeltz
Dany Khosrovani
William and Kay
Koplovitz
Laura Pels
Ben Rauch and Margaret
Scott
Mr. and Mrs. Gerald
Schoenfeld

Patrons
Arthur Bellinzoni
Linda Bialecki and
Douglas Klassen
Catherine Curran
Mr. and Mrs. Robert
Donnalley
William and Ursula
Fairbairn
Mr. and Mrs. Richard
Grand
Sahra Lese
Susan Marks
Mr. and Mrs. Hamish
Maxwell
Jeff and Cynthia Penney
Sylvia Scheuer
Amy Weinstein
Katheryn Williams

Benefactors
Rachael Bail
Mr. and Mrs. Matthew
Chapman
David Day and John
Drummond
T. Richard Fishbein and
Estelle Bender

Jennifer Laing
Imelda Liddiard
Rhonda and Robert
Sherman
Mika Sterling
Chuck Wentzel and Kevin
Fullerton

Members
Jon Armstrong
Eleanor Cicerchi
Christopher Flacke
Nancy Flinn
Rochelle Ohrstrom
Mr. and Mrs. Daniel
Okrent
Tim Runion and Vipul
Nishawala
David and Patricia
Smalley

American Friends
Development Director
Timothy Runion
Tel: +1 212 408 0465

PROGRAMME SUPPORTERS

The Royal Court (English Stage Company Ltd) receives its principal funding from London Arts. It is also supported financially by a wide range of private companies and public bodies and earns the remainder of its income from the box office and its own trading activities.
The Royal Borough of Kensington & Chelsea gives an annual grant to the Royal Court Young Writers' Programme and the Affiliation of London Government provides project funding for a number of play development initiatives.

The Jerwood Charitable Foundation continues to support new plays by new playwrights through the Jerwood New Playwrights series. Since 1993 the A.S.K. Theater Projects of Los Angeles has funded a Playwrights' Programme at the theatre. Bloomberg Mondays, the Royal Court's reduced price ticket scheme, is supported by Bloomberg.
Over the past seven years the BBC has supported the Gerald Chapman Fund for directors.

AWARDS FOR
THE ROYAL COURT

Terry Johnson's Hysteria won the 1994 Olivier Award for Best Comedy, and also the Writers' Guild Award for Best West End Play. Kevin Elyot's My Night with Reg won the 1994 Writers' Guild Award for Best Fringe Play, the Evening Standard Award for Best Comedy, and the 1994 Olivier Award for Best Comedy. Joe Penhall was joint winner of the 1994 John Whiting Award for Some Voices. Sebastian Barry won the 1995 Writers' Guild Award for Best Fringe Play, the Critics' Circle Award and the 1995 Lloyds Private Banking Playwright of the Year Award for The Steward of Christendom. Jez Butterworth won the 1995 George Devine Award, the Writers' Guild New Writer of the Year Award, the Evening Standard Award for Most Promising Playwright and the Olivier Award for Best Comedy for Mojo.

The Royal Court was the overall winner of the 1995 Prudential Award for the Arts for creativity, excellence, innovation and accessibility. The Royal Court Theatre Upstairs won the 1995 Peter Brook Empty Space Award for innovation and excellence in theatre.

Michael Wynne won the 1996 Meyer-Whitworth Award for The Knocky. Martin McDonagh won the 1996 George Devine Award, the 1996 Writers' Guild Best Fringe Play Award, the 1996 Critics' Circle Award and the 1996 Evening Standard Award for Most Promising Playwright for The Beauty Queen of Leenane. Marina Carr won the 19th Susan Smith Blackburn Prize (1996/7) for Portia Coughlan. Conor McPherson won the 1997 George Devine Award, the 1997 Critics' Circle Award and the 1997 Evening Standard Award for Most Promising Playwright for The Weir. Ayub Khan-Din won the 1997 Writers' Guild Awards for Best West End Play and Writers' Guild New Writer of the Year and the 1996 John Whiting Award for East is East (co-production with Tamasha).

At the 1998 Tony Awards, Martin McDonagh's The Beauty Queen of Leenane (co-production with Druid Theatre Company) won four awards including Garry Hynes for Best Director and was nominated for a further two. Eugene Ionesco's The Chairs (co-production with Theatre de Complicite) was nominated for six Tony awards. David Hare won the 1998 Time Out Live Award for Outstanding Achievement and six awards in New York including the Drama League, Drama Desk and New York Critics Circle Award for Via Dolorosa. Sarah Kane won the 1998 Arts Foundation Fellowship in Playwriting. Rebecca Prichard won the 1998 Critics' Circle Award for Most Promising Playwright for Yard Gal (co-production with Clean Break).

Conor McPherson won the 1999 Olivier Award for Best New Play for The Weir. The Royal Court won the 1999 ITI Award for Excellence in International Theatre. Sarah Kane's Cleansed was judged Best Foreign Language Play in 1999 by Theater Heute in Germany. Gary Mitchell won the 1999 Pearson Best Play Award for Trust. Rebecca Gilman was joint winner of the 1999 George Devine Award and won the 1999 Evening Standard Award for Most Promising Playwright for The Glory of Living.

Roy Williams and Gary Mitchell were joint winners of the George Devine Award 2000 for Most Promising Playwright for Lift Off and The Force of Change respectively. At the Barclays Theatre Awards 2000 presented by the TMA, Richard Wilson won the Best Director Award for David Gieselmann's Mr Kolpert and Jeremy Herbert won the Best Designer Award for Sarah Kane's 4.48 Psychosis. Gary Mitchell won the Evening Standard's Charles Wintour Award 2000 for Most Promising Playwright for The Force of Change. Stephen Jeffreys' I Just Stopped by to See The Man won an AT&T: On Stage Award 2000. David Eldridge's Under the Blue Sky won the Time Out Live Award 2001 for Best New Play in the West End. Leo Butler won the George Devine Award 2001 for Most Promising Playwright for Redundant. Roy Williams won the Evening Standard's Charles Wintour Award 2001 for Most Promising Playwright for Clubland. Grae Cleugh won the 2001 Olivier Award for Most Promising Playwright for Fucking Games.

In 1999, the Royal Court won the European theatre prize New Theatrical Realities, presented at Taormina Arte in Sicily, for its efforts in recent years in discovering and producing the work of young British dramatists.

ROYAL COURT BOOKSHOP

The bookshop offers a wide range of playtexts and theatre books, with over 1,000 titles. Located in the downstairs Bar and Food area, the bookshop is open Monday to Saturday, afternoons and evenings.

Many Royal Court playtexts are available for just £2 including works by Harold Pinter, Caryl Churchill, Rebecca Gilman, Martin Crimp, Sarah Kane, Conor McPherson, Ayub Khan-Din, Timberlake Wertenbaker and Roy Williams.

For information on titles and special events, Email: bookshop@royalcourttheatre.com
Tel: 020 7565 5024

FOR THE ROYAL COURT

JERWOOD
NEW PLAYWRIGHTS

Since 1993 Jerwood New Playwrights have contributed to some of the Royal Court's most successful productions, including SHOPPING AND FUCKING by Mark Ravenhill (co-production with Out of Joint), EAST IS EAST by Ayub Khan-Din (co-production with Tamasha), THE BEAUTY QUEEN OF LEENANE by Martin McDonagh (co-production with Druid Theatre Company), THE WEIR by Conor McPherson, REAL CLASSY AFFAIR by Nick Grosso, THE FORCE OF CHANGE by Gary Mitchell, ON RAFTERY'S HILL by Marina Carr (co-production with Druid Theatre Company), 4.48 PSYCHOSIS by Sarah Kane, UNDER THE BLUE SKY by David Eldridge, PRESENCE by David Harrower, HERONS by Simon Stephens, CLUBLAND by Roy Williams, REDUNDANT by Leo Butler, NIGHTINGALE AND CHASE by Zinnie Harris, FUCKING GAMES by Grae Cleugh and BEDBOUND by Enda Walsh. This season Jerwood New Playwrights are supporting THE PEOPLE ARE FRIENDLY by Michael Wynne.

The Jerwood Charitable Foundation is a registered charity dedicated to imaginative and responsible funding and sponsorship of the arts, education, design and other areas of human endeavour and excellence.

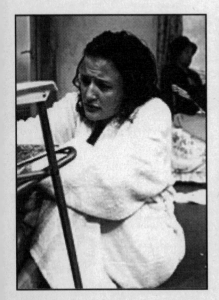

REDUNDANT by Leo Butler
(photo: Ivan Kyncl)

EAST IS EAST by Ayub Khan-Din
(photo: Robert Day)

Michael Wynne
The People Are Friendly

ff

faber and faber

First published in 2002
by Faber and Faber Limited
3 Queen Square London WC1N 3AU
Published in the United States by Faber and Faber Inc.
an affiliate of Farrar, Straus and Giroux LLC, New York

Typeset by Country Setting, Kingsdown, Kent CT14 8ES
Printed in England by Mackays of Chatham plc, Chatham, Kent

A CIP record for this book is available
from the British Library

0-571-21597-1

2 4 6 8 10 9 7 5 3 1

For Billy Wynne

Characters

Michelle Hanlon

Robert Williamson

Kathleen Hanlon

Donna Hanlon

Brian Yates

Eddie Yates

John Hanlon

Kirsty Hanlon

It is the summer of 2001.

Act One

The living room of a large Victorian house. All bare floorboards, high ceilings and cornices. The walls bare, the wallpaper all stripped off. It looks very much like the inhabitants have just moved in, but they have tried to make it look as homely as possible. There are a large sofa and armchair to the right of the room, in front of it a low coffee table on wheels, covered in newspapers and magazines. A sideboard with a CD player on it. Next to the sofa is a large cream rug with a big bag of barbecue charcoal sitting on it. There are two doors on the upper wall: one to the left which leads to the kitchen, another which leads to a large hallway. To the left leads to the kitchen and the stairs. To the right leads to the front door. We can see another door across the hallway which leads into another room. Next to the kitchen on the left-hand wall is a set of french windows which lead into a garden, a small table in front. Ivy grows round the frame, the doors are open. Just out of view is an unlit barbecue. The sun shines bright through the window, it is late afternoon. Birds sing in the garden. It appears to be the perfect peaceful country house.

Robert lies asleep on the sofa. He is fully dressed with his feet on the coffee table. The faint sound of keys in the lock of the front door. The door opens. Michelle is back from the shops. She has a northern accent but it's hard to pinpoint exactly where she's from. Robert is well spoken.

Michelle I'm back.

Robert wakes up. He jumps up quickly, disorientated, and wipes dribble off his chin.

(*shouting down the long echoey hall*) I got a bit carried away. (*She drops two full plastic bags of shopping off at the front door.*) I'll just get the rest from the car. They'll be here soon. I can't smell the barbecue.

Robert Shit!

Michelle goes back out to the car.
   Robert moves to go into the garden but realises he needs matches. He bounds into the kitchen and picks up a large box of cook's matches. He dashes to the garden to light the barbecue. He opens the box to get a match out on the way. But he's holding the box upside down and they all fall on the floor.

Shit!

He scrambles about on the floor picking them up and putting them back into the box. Michelle comes back into the hall and dumps another set of plastic bags.

Michelle I hope they're hungry. It didn't look like that much in the trolley. I've bought some more bubbly. You can never have enough. Will you give me a hand?

Robert I'm quite busy here.

Michelle I'll just get the last lot.

She goes back out to the car. Robert gets all the matches back into the box, takes one out and goes outside forcefully to the barbecue. He comes straight back in.

Robert Charcoal?

He spots the bag. He picks up the bag of charcoal from the top and heads to the door. The bottom of the bag bursts open and the charcoal empties all over the cream rug. He stands still holding the paper bag, staring at the mountain of coal on the floor. He puts

*the empty bag down and runs into the kitchen. He
scrambles about looking for another container,
opening cupboards and looking through the boxes
on the floor.*

*He comes back in with a plastic mop-bucket. He
unclips the wringer part from the top and throws it
back into the kitchen. He quickly transfers the bricks
into the bucket, scooping them up in his hands. He
picks them all up and throws in the burst bag too.
He picks up the bucket but sees the large black sooty
mark on the rug. He lets out a yelp. He puts the
bucket to one side and flails about not knowing what
to do. Michelle comes into the hall with the last of the
shopping. She closes the door behind her.*

Michelle That's everything.

*Michelle heads down the hall. Robert moves to pick
up the rug but he sees that his hands are black with
soot.*

Just met the bloke from next door. Seems nice. Quite
young and trendy. Got a beautiful BMW. I think he
could be an architect or something like that. He saw the
champagne and asked when he's invited. D'you think we
should ask him round?

*Michelle passes by the door to the hall. Robert runs
into the kitchen and washes his hands.*

I do like it round here. (*She enters the kitchen and puts
the bags down on the floor.*) What you doing?

*She heads back down the hall for the next load.
Robert comes back into the living room.*

Robert Just getting ready.

Michelle What are we going to do with this hall? It's so
dark, it depresses me every time I come in.

Robert looks at the rug and round the room, not knowing what to do.

How long do you think this wallpaper's been up here? Shitty brown walls with shitty brown flowers on it.

Michelle passes back past the door and drops another load, which includes a bunch of flowers, into the kitchen. She heads back for the final load.
Robert spots the coffee table. He wheels it quickly over the stain.

All white. And a big mirror. Reflects the light and you can check your hair on the way out. I've got to stop watching those makeover programmes.

He picks up the bucket of coal as Michelle walks into the room carrying the last of the shopping. He breathes a sigh of relief.

What *are* you doing?

Robert (*casual*) Just tidying up.

Michelle Have you moved the coffee table?

Robert Yeah, more space for other guests.

Michelle looks at it, she's not sure.

What else have you bought? I thought we cleared out all the shops yesterday.

Michelle I only went in for some extra bits, little things. And you know I said I wasn't going to do proper, nice food, the stuff we like, because they won't eat it. Well, I thought that's actually really patronising . . .

Robert But true . . .

Michelle And also the old way I used to treat my family and I'm not going to be like that any more. Just assuming they won't like – (*She takes out a packet from the bag.*) – haloumi cheese . . .

Robert They won't.

Michelle No, they won't. I don't like it, why should they? It's like rubber. But I've got other stuff that I bet you they've never tried before . . .

Robert That's patronising.

Michelle Or they probably eat all the time. Just you wait and see, I bet you we'll be surprised. There's peanuts and pickled onions if they won't eat any of this. How's the barbecue getting on? Is it that environmentally friendly coal that doesn't give off much smoke?

Robert You've just caught me mid –

Michelle (*she notices the coal in the mop bucket*) What's the coal doing in there?

Robert There must have been some damp in the basement. The bag had all rotted, I had to transfer it to somewhere . . .

Michelle There's no damp. The survey said there's no damp.

Robert Maybe the bag was damp, wet.

Michelle (*she looks at her watch*) Have I been gone that long? I've been gone hours and you still haven't even lit it? They're meant to be here now.

Robert It's all under control. I'm in charge of the barbecue. You're not going to worry about anything. Look, I set up the table and chairs down the bottom of the garden.

Michelle Well, they're no good if there's nothing to eat at them.

Robert There is now you've bought all that –

Michelle This is really important for me . . .

Robert I know, I know. I'll light it . . .

Michelle I want everything to be right, to be perfect.

Robert (*wanting to go*) So let's . . . just do it. (*Robert goes out into the garden.*)

Michelle They'll be late. They're always late.

Robert (*coming in*) These firelighters are damp, they're never going to light.

Michelle That's what they're meant to be like. It's oil, petrol on them to make them light.

Robert Should they be green and furry, though?

Michelle I'll do it. (*Michelle takes the box of firelighters off Robert and goes outside.*)

Robert We'll use newspaper. (*Robert picks up the Saturday* Guardian *from the coffee table. He picks up the main section.*)

Michelle I haven't read that yet.

Robert We buy it every day and neither of us reads it. I just read the headlines and the bits under the photographs.

Michelle I'm going to start reading it properly.

Robert Which bit don't you want? Review?

Michelle No, keep that, I'd like to see what's on round here, there's a Tate Gallery in Liverpool, you know. Oh, ee are, they're lighting. (*the firelighters*)

Robert Travel?

Michelle There's a special thing about South America, I want to have a look at it.

Robert Jobs?

Michelle Yeah.

Robert You've just got a new one.

Michelle I meant for you.

Robert Ha, ha.

Michelle (*the firelighters*) No, they've gone out again.

Robert Money?

Michelle Yeah.

Robert What for?

Michelle It had something about investing in second homes.

Robert We've just bought this, isn't one enough?

Michelle (*coming in with the firelighters in her hand*) Yeah, they're damp. They'll have been sitting outside that garage for months getting pissed on. I think the coals are okay. Use the sport. I never read that.

Robert I want to have a look at that.

Michelle You?

Robert I was going to read up about football, so I'd have something to talk to your dad about.

Michelle You can't read the paper once and think that you know all about football.

Robert That's how I get all my other opinions.

Michelle There's loads you can talk to me dad about, he hasn't got just one specialist subject.

Robert What else then?

Michelle Local history. Politics. I told you he used to be big in the trade unions, when he was working.

Robert I was brought up being told never to talk about politics. And religion.

Michelle No, me mum's religion. Me dad's politics. Stick to that and you'll be fine.

Robert We can talk about your new job. What do you think he'll say?

Michelle He'll be fine. (*Michelle sees that Robert still has the newspaper in his hand.*) Just use the bloody sports pages, get it lit. It's time. They're going to be here now. I haven't done anything. All this food to do. I've got to change. I'm not convinced about the coffee table.

Robert Leave it! It's fine.

Michelle Okay, okay. I'll just go and get changed.

Robert heads towards the barbecue with the newspaper, he looks at the sports page.

Robert (*revising*) The manager of Liverpool is Gerard Houllier.

Michelle He supports Tranmere Rovers.

Robert scrumples the paper up into a ball and goes out to the garden. The doorbell rings.

They're here. We've got to get rid of that bell.

Robert (*coming back in*) Go on then.

Michelle You get it. I've got to . . . (*Michelle picks up the shopping and dashes into the kitchen.*)

Robert I'm just . . . I don't even know them.

Robert goes to get the front door. Michelle comes back in with the flowers in a tall vase. She puts it on the table by the door, stands back to look at it – it's fine. She sees the boxes of books are still there, tuts and pushes them more against the wall. She quickly tidies up the papers and magazines on the coffee table.

Kathleen steps into the living room, not sure where she's going. Robert goes into the kitchen and empties the shopping bags.

Kathleen Through here?

Robert Yeah, yeah.

Michelle Yes, Mother. Come on.

Kathleen Hiya, love. Oh it just gets better. Look at this.

Michelle Hiya, Mum. (*Michelle gives her a hug and a kiss.*) It's good to see you.

Kathleen I thought I had the wrong house. I've spoken to him on the phone but I had a completely different face in me head. I was certain he had curly hair. I didn't wanna be late, I know how you hate us always being late. Is this place yours?

Michelle No, we've just broken in. Is it just you? Where's me dad?

Kathleen He's at work. He doesn't finish till seven.

Michelle He's got a job, that's good.

Kathleen Is it?

Michelle Where's he working?

Kathleen Down at the car park in town. Checking people have paid and displayed. Don't ask. (*looking round*) I can't believe this place, it's like something off *Upstairs, Downstairs*. We got y' a bottle of wine. That's what you do, isn't it? (*Kathleen hands her the wine in a plastic Threshers bag.*)

Michelle You didn't have to.

Kathleen Don't you want to look at it, see that it's all right?

Michelle It'll be fine.

Kathleen It wasn't a cheap one. Although it was on special offer. It's white.

Michelle drops it into the kitchen.

Just look at this place and look at you.

Michelle I know, I meant to get changed.

Kathleen Your hair, what happened to it? Where did it all go?

Michelle This? I had it all cut off last year. I've seen you since then.

Kathleen It's about eighteen months we haven't seen you. Oh, your dad loved your long hair, he'll be upset.

Michelle It can't be.

Kathleen It is. We didn't see you this last Christmas, you were off, where was it?

Michelle Cuba.

Kathleen And I was starting to think you'd forgotten our phone number.

Michelle Oh thanks, Mum. I know I haven't spoken to you for ages but this year's been mad and then with moving back I didn't phone 'cause I wanted it to be a surprise. And there's just no time in London. You're so busy running about, before you know it you've been living there twelve years.

Kathleen And this quick phone call, 'I'm back, living up the road and I'm having a barbecue on Saturday.' You've been here a few days, why didn't you come and see us?

Michelle I wanted to make an occasion of it. Special.

Kathleen You always have to do things different, don't you?

Michelle Well, I'm back now, so . . .

Robert (*coming in*) Can I get you a drink, Kathleen?

Kathleen A tea'd be nice, love.

Michelle Have a drink drink. A beer, a wine? We've got some fizzy but we'll open that when everyone gets here.

Kathleen Oh I'll tell y' what. I'll have half a glass of beer topped up with lemo. I'm quite thirsty.

Robert (*going back into the kitchen*) Coming up.

Kathleen Isn't he lovely. (*having a look round*) How can you afford a place like this? Have you robbed a bank or won the lottery?

Michelle We sold the flat in Clapham and we bought this for . . . Well, it was less than the flat.

Kathleen No.

Michelle I know, a tiny two-bedroom flat for a five-bedroom house. The house prices in London are ridiculous. It needs some work doing to it but we got a good deal.

Kathleen Five bedrooms? It's a mansion. What are y' gonna do with five bedrooms?

Michelle I just like the idea of living in a big house. Robert's going to use one bedroom as an office to write his book. And we do see it as a family house.

Kathleen You're not . . . are you? Oh, I thought you were looking a bit . . .

Michelle I'm not pregnant.

Kathleen Oh. Are you sure?

Michelle Yes. It's these trousers, I'll go and change.

Kathleen No, no, you look fine. (*changing the subject*) Is that a dildo rail?

Robert comes in with the beer, he nearly drops the drink.

Michelle What?

Kathleen There, the dildo rail.

Michelle Dado, dado rail.

Kathleen Are you sure? I thought . . . (*thinking*) Well, what's that then?

Robert (*handing her the drink*) Kathleen.

Kathleen Ta, love. I like them, I tried to get your father to put one in the living room but he thought they'd look fake in a house built in the sixties.

Robert heads back to the kitchen, trying to keep his laughter in.

Michelle We're thinking of making a lot of changes, aren't we?

Robert Mmm, yes.

Michelle Maybe knocking through here, moving the kitchen back into the basement. We've started decorating in here – well, we've stripped all the dodgy wallpaper off. (*saying it loudly for his benefit*) Robert was going to paint it yesterday. We ripped the carpet up and the floorboards aren't too bad.

18

Kathleen (*looking round*) I'm scared to touch anything. You've got some lovely stuff. Oh, those flowers, they look real.

Michelle They are real.

Kathleen (*she goes to the windows*) Look at the garden.

Michelle It's all a bit wild and overgrown, but I quite like it like that. I love the way it slopes down to the trees and the gazebo thing at the bottom. I think it's a gazebo. And look, we've got a garden table and chairs in it – that's where we're going to eat later.

Kathleen Oh, it's wonderful.

Michelle If you stand up here the view's amazing. You should have seen the sunset last night. And look – (*Michelle points.*) See.

Kathleen I don't know what I'm looking for.

Michelle Look, through the trees, in the middle. The estate.

Kathleen Oh God. Is that the estate? Now would you look at that.

Michelle Isn't it great. I was trying to see if I could see ours, I mean yours, or Donna's. There's the church. So where are you?

Kathleen Isn't it funny, looking at it like this, it's like Lego. Ooh, ee are, see that burnt-out house. That's in the same row as Donna's. Aah, the mother and two kids killed, burnt to a crisp. They think it was either one of the kids had been smoking in bed or her fella, well her ex, set fire to the place, thinking the kids were out. I know it was him. He had one of those restraining orders too. Wasn't meant to go near them, after that business on Boxing Day. Never liked him, got a moustache like a Mexican. He's disappeared, hasn't he. The eldest daughter was lucky, she'd been arrested for drunk and disorderly in town and they kept her in the cells overnight. She says those twelve pints saved her life.

Michelle So where are . . .

Kathleen They had a smoke alarm too. Or what they thought was a smoke alarm. Some little toerag had been selling industrial air-fresheners as smoke alarms door to door. He'd taken the smelly bit out. So that'll be Donna's, two along. There. And we're four rows behind. Look, there we are with the red door, you can see us. You'll be able to know if we're in or not.

Michelle That's what clinched it, being so near to you lot.

Kathleen So are you gonna give me the tour or what?

Michelle Yeah, come on. Robert, have you lit the barbecue? It's not even warm.

Robert (*coming in*) You asked me to answer the door.

Michelle (*to Kathleen*) Shall we start at the top?

Robert goes outside. Michelle and Kathleen go through to the hall.

Kathleen Just look at these stairs.

Michelle and Kathleen go upstairs.

Robert Bloody light, you bastard. (*Robert comes back in and picks up a section of newspaper.*) Jobs. Won't be needing that. (*He tears out a few pages and screws them up into a ball. He goes out into the garden. He scrunches more paper. He strikes a match.*) Come on, light, light you stupid thing.

The doorbell rings.

Do you want to get that, Michelle? Come on, that's it, now light the other one. Come on, let's all come together and make one big flame. That's it, now stay lit, you stupid . . .

The doorbell rings again. Robert comes through and goes to the front door.

I'm coming, I'm coming. (*shouting up the stairs*) Couldn't you have got it? I'm trying to light this sodding barbecue. (*Robert opens the door.*) Hello? Come on in. Come on in. Just through there.

Donna comes into the living room, followed by Brian.

Donna This is the rest of my gang. Brian, me fella.

Brian All right, mate.

Robert Pleased to meet you.

Donna Eddie and the baby. (*She wheels a three-wheeler pram by the hall door.*) If we just leave him there he'll be fine. We'll know when he's awake.

Robert Michelle's just showing your mum round.

Brian (*looking round*) Fuckin' hell, it's the Amytville house.

Donna Eddie? Where is he?

Eddie appears in the kitchen doorway.

Come and sit down 'ere, love.

Eddie comes through and sits down on the sofa. He's a very angelic-looking child. He sits still and quiet.

Donna We got y' a box of Miniature Heroes and a bottle of tequila. I sent him the shop and told him to get something classy to drink and he gets tequila.

Brian It was either that or Malibu, that was the only stuff out of the way of the cameras.

Robert (*not sure if it's a joke or not*) Oh, right.

Donna And I asked for Celebrations, they're much nicer. These'll have to do. Steer clear of the Mini-Picnics, though, they're like dog chews.

Robert Thanks for that. (*He takes them into the kitchen.*)

Donna Where did she find him?

Brian (*looking round*) They must have a few bob 'ere. This place is boss.

Donna It's cold.

Brian The doors are open.

Donna No, I mean I can feel . . .

Brian If you start that I'm going home.

Robert (*coming back in*) Do sit down.

Donna We thought we'd never get to meet you, that she'd made you up.

Robert I was always working or busy when she came up to visit. But now I'm here for good.

Brian Eh, great place you've got 'ere, eh, Rob. It's a bit like our house, isn't it, Don?

Donna (*sitting down next to Eddie*) I think this is a bit smaller.

Robert Can I get you a drink?

Brian I wouldn't say no.

Robert There's beer, wine, spirits . . .

Brian Where shall I start? Let's have a look.

Robert and Brian go through to the kitchen.

I'll get something for her.

Donna has a nose around. Michelle comes down the stairs. She's changed into a dress.

Michelle I thought I could hear someone. (*She looks into the pram.*) Hello? Aah, is this Kirsty's baby? He's beautiful. Hiya, Don.

Donna Oh, hiya.

Michelle gives Donna a hug and a kiss.

Michelle How old's Kirsty, she must be . . .

Donna She's sixteen now.

Michelle God, that means . . .

Donna She's the same age as when I had her.

Michelle Funny that, isn't it?

Donna Fuckin' hilarious. She's left it late, most girls have them at twelve now. Get them out the way.

Michelle So you're a grandmother?

Donna Yeah, thanks for that.

Michelle (*looking at him*) What's he called again?

Donna Reinar.

Michelle Reinar, it's such an unusual name. I've never heard it before.

Donna You won't have, she made it up.

Michelle Oh, right.

Donna Bloody stupid if you ask me.

Michelle Aah, he's fast asleep.

Donna So he should be, he had me up all night screaming the place down.

Michelle I bet you love looking after him.

Donna Someone's got to, it's either me or me mum that gets lumbered with him.

Michelle I would've liked to have seen Kirsty.

Donna Oh, she is coming. She's just topping up her fake tan and applying another twenty layers of make-up.

Michelle The last time I saw her she was just a little girl. I bet she's grown up a lot.

Donna Oh yeah, she looks about forty-five now.

Michelle And little Eddie. Look at the size of you, you're not little any more. You all right there?

Eddie looks at her. He doesn't say anything.

You're very quiet.

Donna He is now.

Michelle Are you shy?

Donna Naah, he doesn't speak, do y' kid?

Michelle He can't speak?

Donna Oh, I'm sure he can, the doctors say there's nothing wrong with him. He just doesn't.

Michelle Can he hear?

Donna Oh yeah, he's always listening. Just mute. It's like someone pressed the mute button on the remote one day and that was it. You forget he's here, it's great.

Michelle Do you want to have a look round?

Donna In a minute.

Brian (*coming out of the kitchen with his and Donna's drinks*) There's *some* booze in there. I told you it was worth coming.

> *Robert follows him out of the kitchen with a drink for Michelle, he hands it to her.*

Robert Just help yourself to whatever.

Donna Don't worry, he will.

Michelle Hiya, Brian. How are you doing?

Brian On top of the world. All the better for seeing you.

Donna D'you know who lived 'ere before?

Robert A Mrs Winstanley.

Michelle Some old woman. She'd been here for years. Hence the wacky wallpaper. I don't know when it was last decorated.

Donna She lived 'ere on her own?

Michelle Yeah, I think she had a large family, but all the kids moved away down south . . .

Donna Sounds familiar.

Michelle And her husband died and she was left here alone.

Donna Did she spend a lot of time in 'ere?

Robert Apparently she was just living in this one room, that's why the rest of the house is in such a bad way. She had her bed put in here so she could see the garden.

Michelle What are you getting at?

Donna Did she die in this room, because I'm getting . . .

Brian Oh, don't start, Don.

Donna I wouldn't say it if I didn't but I . . . Did she?

Michelle No, she died in hospital, didn't she, Robert?

Robert Oh yes, in hospital.

Michelle The snotty woman with the Land-Rover across the road told him.

Donna Maybe it's further back but I'm definitely getting a feeling . . . that something's happened in this room.

Brian Ignore her. She doesn't know what she's talking about.

Donna I didn't say I was psychic, just that I can sense something.

Brian Eh, there was this cracking thing on Channel Five the other night where they found all these bones under the floorboards of a house and they thought a serial killer had lived there.

Robert I saw that. Oh, that bit where they found the skeleton of a pregnant woman and you could see the baby inside her too.

Brian It put me right off me tea. Anyway, it wasn't a serial killer, it turns out they'd built the street on a graveyard, y'know, like in *Poltergeist*.

Donna Y' see that's what happened on our estate, they built it on a cemetery.

Michelle Did they?

Brian No.

Donna It's not in any records or anything, but I think it was back in the Dark Ages and it was just a small one. There's definitely something going on. I've had a few experiences, seen things. Y' know, stuff moving about by itself. You make yourself a ham buttie and y' turn your back and it's moved somewhere else.

Brian Well, why does it just happen to you, eh? Why don't I see any of this?

Donna The spirits can't be arsed with you, can they? They know you don't believe. Anyway, you don't do anything. What's it gonna do? Change channels for y'?

Brian It's a load of bollocks.

Donna I'll tell y' who has seen it. (*She turns to Eddie.*) D'you wanna go and look at the garden?

He doesn't move.

Go on. Go and have a run round before I give you y' pills.

He gets up and walks out into the garden.

It's me and him that it happens to most. I think that maybe he saw something and it scared him so much he could never speak again.

Brian He stopped speaking when he went on the tablets. He doesn't say anything because he's drugged up to the eyeballs.

Donna Well, how d'you account for what's happened in the rest of the street? Eh?

Brian It'll be something to do with the water.

Donna They've checked that out.

Robert What is it?

Donna All the pets have died. There's only Snowy, Mrs Elliot's cocker spaniel, left, and that's under twenty-four-hour surveillance. She's even getting CCTV cameras fitted in its kennel – her son nicked them from the old

Kwiksave. Although how you can steal security cameras I don't know. It all started with Margy Stanner's tropical fish from work. I said I'd look after them while she went on holiday. She'd won two weeks to Disneyland in *Take a Break*. Anyway, she brought her tank round, we were looking after her fish, beautiful they were, and they started dying. Not all together, but one by one. We'd come down every morning and there'd be another one floating arse-up. Ten there was, dead in ten days. She's still not talking to me. But then in the street, everyone's pets started dying. Mandy Keaney's two cats, Benson and Hedges. Dead. The Parkers' labrador. The Gomersawls' gerbils. Even Tracey's pet duck Arthur. All dead. The whole street wiped out. And I wouldn't give Snowy much longer, he's about three hundred in dog years anyway.

Kathleen (*coming out of the kitchen*) I've already told y'. Father Wilson will come down and do y' an exorcism. He's very good at them. He got rid of that thing from Brenda's loft. Ooh, let's have a look at the garden. (*She goes out to the garden.*)

Donna Y' see, at first I thought it was a friendly spirit. I thought it was just playing games with me. But now it's taking the piss. And I can sense things when I go into other people's houses. If there's a presence or a spirit that's not at ease.

Michelle Don't say you can feel something in here.

Donna There's something about this room.

Michelle (*to Robert*) Mrs Winstanley died in here, didn't she? That's what the cow across the road told you that you wouldn't tell me.

Robert No, she was telling me about the tree they had cut down in the front garden, the roots were growing under the house.

Donna He's a crap liar him, isn't he?

Michelle It's embarrassing.

Robert I thought that was good. I was proud of that.

Michelle So she died in here?

Robert Yeah.

Donna Oh, God.

Michelle Oh, great.

Brian It is Amytville.

Donna And I bet she was dead for some time.

Michelle She was, wasn't she?

Robert No, she died with all her family round her and they took her straight to the funeral parlour.

Michelle (*knowing he's lying*) How long did she rot here for?

Robert Six months.

Michelle Oh, great.

Donna I could feel that.

Brian Get away.

Robert Apparently, they only found out when the house got broken into and the neighbours heard the screams of the burglar when he saw her. She was all skin and bones.

Donna That'd put you off robbing, wouldn't it.

Brian I bet y' it was like something out of *Indiana Jones*. Where they're lost in some temple and they shine the torch and you see this rotten skull with all maggots and beetles crawling out of the eye sockets.

Robert (*enjoying it*) Oh, yeah.

Michelle D'you mind?

Donna I thought that sort of thing only happened on our estate. I think the record's nine months.

Michelle (*to Robert*) What did she die of?

Robert They don't know. But she died with a shocked expression on her face like she'd seen something which had scared her to death.

Michelle That's not funny.

Robert Isn't it?

Michelle No.

Robert (*going out*) I'll get back to the barbecue.

Michelle Just think, spending your last days alone, with no one even knowing or caring that you'd died.

Donna You'd think if she was rich she'd have loads of people round her. Nurses and cleaners and stuff.

Michelle Have I bought a haunted house? What d'you think I should do?

Brian Just ignore her, that's what I do.

Donna You might be fine. If I see or feel anything I'll let you know. You could get me mum to sprinkle some holy water about.

Kathleen (*coming back in*) This house is wonderful. Have you seen the basement, Donna? There's even a place where the maid would have slept.

Donna You can sleep there when you come to stay.

Kathleen I won't need to, it's got five bedrooms. Five. And there's a room right at the top of the house where you can see the river. It was built by this shipping bloke.

Michelle This whole road was built by the shipping owners, you'll see if you look at some of the other houses, little anchors and ships on the brickwork.

Kathleen And you know what? Guess what you can see from the top of the garden?

Donna The Eiffel Tower?

Kathleen You can see the estate. Your house and our house.

Donna Get some conifers in there quick. You don't wanna be paying good money to be living 'ere and all you can see is where you grew up.

Michelle I like it.

Kathleen I think they'll be able to see whether we're in or not.

Donna Lucky for them.

Brian Remind me to not walk round in the nuddy, she'll be watching us.

Donna I can tell y' now, there's nothing to see.

Michelle *(to Robert)* Shall we open the fizzy now?

Robert *(coming in from the garden)* I'm just lighting the barbecue, do you want . . .

Michelle I thought it was lit.

Robert It keeps going out.

Michelle Well, do the drinks and then we'll try and light it again.

Brian D'you want me to have a look? I'm good at getting things to light.

Donna Yeah, it's called arson.

31

Michelle Naah, Robert likes doing it, don't you?

Robert (*going into the kitchen*) Oh yes. It's my favourite thing.

Brian Just give me the nod, 'Chelle, and I'll sort it out for y'. (*shouting through to the kitchen*) Do some nibbles as well.

Michelle Would Eddie like a lemonade or something?

Donna He only drinks Coke or Sunny Delight.

Michelle They're full of additives, them, you know.

Donna I know, but otherwise he won't drink. I've tried everything. Wait until we get round to the food. It's like feeding some rare breed of monkey. He's creating his own eating disorder. He went on hunger strike the other week because I tried to cut out crisps and sweets.

A champagne cork pops in the kitchen.

Michelle What's actually wrong with him? Has he got that attention deficit thing?

Donna Something like that. Half the boys in his class have got it.

Michelle There's so much you can do now. You could try some alternative therapies like homeopathy or cranial massage. There was a piece in the paper about how playing Mozart can unlock some children.

Robert comes through with the drinks on a tray.

Robert Here we are.

Kathleen Ooh, look at this.

Robert passes them around.

Brian I'm glad you came back now, 'Chelle.

Donna Kirsty'll be well pissed off she missed this.

Michelle There's plenty more.

Robert Shall we do a little toast?

Michelle What a good idea.

Robert Right. A toast to . . . new beginnings.

Kathleen That sounds good.

Various cheers, 'New beginnings' and oohs and aahs.

Kathleen Ooh, I like this.

Donna So what's this all about, then? It's like an Agatha Christie. 'I have invited you all here tonight . . .' Who's gonna get bumped off first?

Michelle There's no big deal. I've just come back and I wanted to have a little party, a little do.

Donna But why've you come back?

Kathleen Donna, this is her home, isn't it.

Donna Is it? I thought you'd never come back to live 'ere.

Michelle Do you know what, we'd just both had enough of London. There's great things about living in London but the bad was outweighing the good. (*to Robert*) Wasn't it?

Robert That's where I'm from and I'd had enough of it.

Brian How did she convince you to move up here, eh, Rob?

Robert If anyone needed convincing it was Michelle. I thought it was a great idea. I needed some space to write my book and Michelle had just been –

33

Michelle I needed a change of job.

Robert I'm so glad we've done it, I love it here.

Michelle We were tempted by living over in Liverpool, in the city centre, getting one of those warehouse apartments. But we thought that was a bit of a cliché. Liverpool's changed so much now. There's a new bar or restaurant on every corner. The city's finally found its feet. But then we saw this house and there was no contest. We wanted to be part of a community. A proper house. And I want to be here and see the turn-around in Birkenhead.

Donna I'd like to see that too.

Michelle But it's everything else about London. The Tube. Being jammed up against people's armpits every morning. The dirt. The smell. The crime. Everyone's always running about, tutting, huffing and puffing. And you start doing it yourself. It's got to the point now where if someone's walking slowly in front of me down the street, like they always do, I kick them. Kick them in the back of the heel and then say sorry. Like I didn't do it on purpose, but I just caught them because they were walking so bloody slowly. So they know to either speed up or get out of the way. Can you believe it?

Kathleen You don't do that, do you?

Robert I've seen her do it.

Donna God.

Michelle I've only done it a couple of times.

Donna I wouldn't want to get on the wrong side of you.

Brian Don't mess with Michelle, she's trouble.

Michelle That's the point, it's ridiculous, and all I'm doing is going to work or going the post office. What's

34

the big rush? The other week I was getting off the Tube and everyone was moving really slowly, I started pushing and shouting, 'Don't worry, we've got all day.' I manage to push past and it's only a little old blind woman, isn't it? I felt terrible.

Donna You're a fuckin' nightmare.

Michelle And you couldn't bring up kids in London.

Donna Are you . . .

Kathleen No, she's not.

Michelle But you know what the biggest difference being back is? What you notice straight away?

Brian The smackheads.

Donna The shit jobs.

Kathleen The weather.

Michelle The people.

Kathleen Oh yeah.

Michelle The people are friendlier. You go into a shop and the person in front holds the door open for you. They don't let it smack in your face. And you say thanks. Then if you do it for someone else, they say thanks. And just little things, like being called love when you get your change.

Donna Are you taking the piss?

Michelle You wouldn't believe how much difference to your day someone saying thank you makes. It's about appreciating people.

Donna No one's got anything better to do.

Robert (*going back into the kitchen*) It's true, the bloke in the newsagents is my new best friend.

Michelle People make an effort. No one can be bothered in London and no one trusts anyone. If you went into town here and lost your money and didn't have enough to get home, I bet you if you asked someone they'd lend it to you. In London you wouldn't stand a chance. Everyone's trying to rip everyone else off. The number of times I've been stopped in the street with, 'My wife's just had a baby and I need to get to the hospital, can you lend me ten pounds for the train and I'll give you my address?'

Brian It's only that the smackheads round 'ere don't know those tricks yet. Give them time.

Michelle I also got fed up with how poncey everything was becoming. I felt like I wasn't living in the real world. It's all about what shoes you're wearing and what restaurant you've just been to. All your friends are the same type of people as you and they haven't really got any real problems. I wanted to come back to the real world. London doesn't feel like the real world.

Robert comes in with a tray of food.

Robert Look what the chef just knocked together.

Michelle Great.

Robert puts the food down on the coffee table.

Kathleen God, what's all this?

Michelle Right. That's foccacia cheese, couscous, tabouleh, asparagus, taramasalata, houmous. Olives and stuffed vine leaves.

Donna Welcome to the real world.

Michelle I thought you might not like it, but then I thought you might do. Just get stuck in. It's going to be a while before the barbecue's ready.

Brian (*the stuffed vine leaves*) What are they?

Michelle They're vine leaves stuffed with rice. They're lovely.

Donna They look like they've just slipped out of someone's arse. Six shits on a plate, really healthy ones. Someone who's been on a high-fibre diet.

Michelle I know it all looks a bit different but . . . Go on, who's gonna try some?

Brian I'm saving meself for the barbie.

Michelle You'll be waiting for ever.

Robert You're making the right choice. I can't stand this stuff.

Michelle Well, they're never going to try it now, are they? Olives, anyone?

Donna They taste like salty piss.

Kathleen (*to Michelle*) And you were such a fussy child.

Robert Good job we've got peanuts.

Donna You can't bring them in 'ere.

Robert You don't like peanuts?

Donna Eddie's not allowed, he's allergic. He nearly died once, he went blue. His throat swelled up, he couldn't breathe.

Brian He can play you like a guitar.

Michelle I'll put them in a bowl. He knows not to eat them, doesn't he?

Donna Yeah, but they say you can have a reaction just from the dust.

Michelle Oh, right.

Donna It wouldn't be so bad if it wasn't for me working in the peanut factory. We could have as many peanuts as we want, fill the house up. We could decorate the place with peanut butter. But they're banned. I have to run into the shower as soon as I get in to get rid of the dust.

Brian He knows all this, that's why he threw his little stunt, didn't he?

Donna Leave him alone.

Robert (*with the champagne bottle*) A top-up, anyone?

Brian I thought you'd never ask. They're only small glasses, aren't they?

Michelle Oh God, you know what I couldn't believe. Have you seen what they've done to Atmosphere? A bloody lap-dancing club. The first thing that greets you as you enter Birkenhead is that.

Brian We'll have to get down there, won't we, Rob?

Robert Oh, yeah.

Michelle I don't think Robert would be interested, would you? Would you?

Robert No, it's not for me.

Brian It's only a bit of fun, isn't it? You girls go and see strippers and things like that, don't y'? Y' know, the Chipmunks.

Michelle I hate all that stuff.

Donna Me and the girls from work went to see some American strippers at the Empire last year. What were they called? The GI Joes. Oh, it was crap. Y' didn't even get to see their dicks. It was a rip-off. You should have seen all these woman screaming, I felt ashamed. You could tell they weren't getting it at home.

Kathleen I think that place in town's a disgrace. Women stripping for dirty old men in macs. No wonder church is empty.

Michelle It's really sad, I used to love Atmosphere. (*to Donna*) That's where we first went clubbing, wasn't it? It was free on a Thursday.

Donna I'm glad they closed it down, I hated that place.

Michelle Wasn't that where you met Kirsty's dad?

Donna Yeah. And the rest is history.

Kathleen (*to Michelle*) So are you still working for that estate agent's?

Michelle No, Mother, I haven't worked there for years. I told you when I left there. I've been working as project manager at that architect's overseeing their developments. We did this great shopping centre in Essex. Then I've just done six months at an internet property company, which was interesting . . .

Kathleen You're still doing that? I can't keep up.

Robert She got the sack.

Brian No?

Michelle I did not get the sack. It went bust, so we all got the sack. But I'd had enough of that anyway. And now we're here. After we'd had the idea of moving I put a few feelers out, contacted some job agencies. And this brilliant job came up in Birkenhead. Similar to what I've been doing but more worthwhile, rewarding. So I applied, was interviewed down in London and at first they didn't even know I was from Birkenhead.

Donna That figures.

Michelle But when they found out I think that's what swung it. They wanted someone who knows the place and the people. And I got the job.

    The doorbell rings. Robert goes to get it.

Donna That'll be our Kirsty.

Kathleen Ooh, what is it?

Michelle I've been in this week getting things ready but I start proper on Monday. It is exciting.

Brian Are you running the new lap-dancing club?

    Robert shows John in. He's wearing a green fluorescent jacket, with NCP written across the chest.

Robert We're all through here.

John Bloody hell, the size of it.

Michelle Hiya, Dad.

John Is that you, Michelle? What happened to your hair? You look like a twelve-year-old schoolboy. Come 'ere. (*He kisses her and hugs her.*) It's nice to have you back, girlie.

Kathleen She was always his favourite.

Donna You're not meant to say things like that, Mother.

Kathleen Well, you can be my favourite.

Donna As some sort of consolation prize.

    Michelle and John break apart.

John I can't believe you're living in this street. You've landed on your feet 'ere.

Michelle I suppose so. Have you met Robert, Dad?

John Yeah. Are you having us on? Is this really his house and you're just the cleaner.

Michelle (*enjoying it*) Dad!

John Right, is that barbecue lit?

Kathleen Are you hungry? I thought you were working till . . .

Donna Anyway, go on, Michelle.

John No, we're going to have a ceremonial burning of this bloody jacket. (*He tears it off.*) I gave the hat and armbands to some kids in the street to play with. It was the final straw when some spotty kid called me Bertie Basset. I'm not working there any more. I told them where they can stick their crappy job.

Brian Good on y', J.

Kathleen It was only a matter of time.

Michelle You've left your job? Is that a good idea?

John I'm not doing a crappy job like that at my age, I'm a skilled worker. They can stuff their new deals, I'd rather starve.

Kathleen Well you won't need it any more, will you?

John It's not definite.

Kathleen But I thought . . .

John It's as good as.

Michelle What are you talking about?

John Haven't you heard? It looks like I'm going back to Lairds. They're taking all the old men back on.

Michelle is speechless. Robert looks to her, she can't look at him.

41

Kathleen It's great, isn't it?

Michelle Yeah, yeah.

John You know, you don't think these things will come round again. I thought I'd had all me chances and after the yard closed for the first time, well I don't think any of us thought this would be happening. I haven't got many more years of working left.

Michelle I thought since they got the receivers in last month it was all over.

John That's what everybody thought but it's the best thing that could have happened. It's been bought out by this big international shipping company who wanna build ships. The blokes who took it over when it first closed down just turned it into a repair shop, a mechanic's. You can't be arsing about with bits of ships, you wanna build the whole thing. People will always need ships. That's where the real jobs and money are.

Michelle So . . . when do you start?

John Well, I haven't been given a date. The lads I've spoken to said we should hear something in the next week or so. And because I was one of the last to be laid off, I should be one of the first to go back in. Sid Saunders said he saw a group of people yesterday going round the site, to see what they need to bring in new. They're saying that Tony Blair got all the people round the table and told them what to do. They say he's only interested in the rich fellas down south but no, he's for y' ordinary bloke like me.

Donna I don't know about that. I still can't believe you voted for him, twice.

John Eh, Michelle, you've moved back just at the right time. This town's getting back on its feet, you wait and see. Once we start getting those ships out and we get the men of this town doing proper jobs again and off the streets. Eh, I tell you the future's gonna be good for our little Eddie and Reinar.

Michelle Do you want a drink, Dad?

John I wouldn't say no.

Donna Go on, Michelle. (*to John*) Michelle was just going to tell us about her new job . . .

John It's good news all round.

Kathleen Oh yeah, go on.

Michelle It doesn't matter.

Donna You can't not tell us now.

Michelle I'm going to be working at Cadbury's. On the management side.

Brian Cadbury's?

Donna Is that it?

Michelle They're launching some new products.

Kathleen Ooh, what?

Michelle A new chocolate bar, I shouldn't really talk about it.

Kathleen Ooh, what's in it?

Michelle It's top secret.

Brian You'd be my boss if I wasn't on the sick. I can't believe I'm missing out on that treat.

Michelle I forgot you'd worked there.

Donna Everyone's worked there. (*to Brian*) You could go back tomorrow, there's nothing wrong with y'. They wouldn't have y' back, though.

43

Kathleen Go on, give us a hint, we won't tell anyone. Has it got nuts in it?

Michelle (*snappy*) It's top secret.

Kathleen Okay.

Michelle Dad, come and get some champagne and then I'll show you round.

Michelle and John go into the kitchen. Robert checks on the barbecue.

Donna A top secret chocolate bar. She's taking life a bit seriously, isn't she?

Kathleen Maybe she'll lose her job if it gets out.

Another champagne cork pops.

Donna You come all the way back 'ere to make chocolate biscuits. I'd call that a bit of a step down. How is that more rewarding?

Kathleen Donna, shush.

Donna I need a ciggie.

Donna gets up and heads outside. She offers one to Brian, who follows her out. Michelle and John come out of the kitchen with the bottle and glasses of champagne.

John I'm not really a fan of this champagne.

Brian (*poking his head in*) Come and have a look at this garden, J. It's like the Lake District out 'ere.

John Is it bigger than our postage-stamp patch of grass?

Brian and John go out into the garden. Robert looks in from the barbecue.

Robert What was that all about?

Michelle What could I say?

Kathleen comes over to Michelle with her champagne glass for a top-up. Robert goes back out to the barbecue.

Kathleen I'm getting a taste for this. I'm so pleased for him, y' know, this Lairds job. He's been over the moon.

Michelle Mmm.

Kathleen You wouldn't believe the change in him. Since he first heard the news, just in these past few weeks.

Michelle How did he find out?

Kathleen I don't know. I know he'd spoken to a few of the old men in town. They were the ones who told him. He said there's been a lot of activity there over the last month, as the new bosses come in.

Michelle Can it really re-open?

Kathleen What d'you mean? Why shouldn't it? It has to, 'cause I can't cope much longer with the way things are.

Michelle Oh, Mum, has it been that bad?

Kathleen Oh, Michelle, I've been at me wits' end. You know what he's been like since he lost his job. He was nothing without that. It was bad enough him being on the dole for years. But when they made him take that job, in the bloody car park, or he'd have his benefits cut, well that was it. I'd hear him crying in the bathroom. But if you asked him if he was all right, he'd say yes. You know what he's like, he wouldn't tell me. He'd be down there checking the tickets and he'd see people he knew, blokes he used to work with. They were embarrassed, he was embarrassed. He said he felt like he'd committed a crime, like he was being punished. Put on public show in that stupid green coat. He said

45

he would have preferred the stocks. I had to force him to go to the doctor's. In the end I made an appointment for him meself and just told him to get down there. He went and they convinced him to go on the Prozac.

Michelle Me dad on Prozac?

Kathleen Don't say anything. He'd die if you knew. The only way I could get him to take them was if he took them at the same time as I took mine.

Michelle You're on them too? Oh, Mum . . .

Kathleen No, me HRT. I was a nightmare before I went on them. I was sweating like a rapist. Though there was times when I felt like helping meself to some of his. Going, 'One for you and one for me.' Anyway, he's stopped taking them now. He came home after he'd heard the news and threw them all in the bin. He said he didn't need happy pills any more.

Michelle Why didn't you tell me any of this?

Kathleen I've hardly spoken to you this year. A lot's changed round 'ere.

Michelle You should have called me.

Kathleen What would you have done? Eh? Sent another cheque?

Michelle I thought you appreciated me sending you money.

Kathleen Oh, I do, Michelle you wouldn't believe the difference it makes, but if it's between a cheque for fifty quid every month or seeing you, I'd much rather have you here.

Michelle (*putting her arm round her*) Well, I'm here now.

Kathleen And it's all over, he's fine, so there's nothing to worry about.

John (*coming in from the garden*) I can't believe my daughter's got a house like this. And it's down to chocolate fingers and cream eggs.

Kathleen Let me show you round?

John Can't I sit down first?

Kathleen No, come on. We'll start at the top.

Kathleen and John go upstairs. Brian and Robert come in.

Brian Nothing's happening there, mate. They're never gonna light. You'd have more luck trying to light one of my farts.

Robert I'll nip out and get another bag of coal.

Michelle This is going to take for ever.

Robert I'll go to Sainsbury's. I'll be there and back in ten minutes.

Michelle gives him a look.

I know where it is. It's right out of here and straight down towards town.

Michelle It's in completely the other direction.

Brian I'll show him. Come on.

Donna (*coming back in*) We won't be seeing those two again.

Robert and Brian go out. Eddie appears in the doorway. He watches Michelle.

Michelle It's all going wrong.

Donna Sit down and shut up.

Donna tops their drinks up and sits down on the sofa. Michelle is very aware of Eddie watching.

Michelle (*to Eddie*) Have you seen the cat?

Eddie looks at her, blank.

(*to Donna*) There's a cat which comes in the garden. We've called it Welcome. It was the first thing we saw when we got here. Does he like cats?

Donna Oh yeah. Go and look for the cat, Eddie.

He watches Michelle for a second then goes back into the garden.

Michelle Is he all right?

Donna Yeah. Is he freaking you out?

Michelle No, no. A bit.

Donna He's fine. (*to Eddie*) Can't you see it? Keep looking. Go down the bottom.

Pause.

Michelle I didn't mean it like that. We have tried but it just hasn't happened yet. We've got to give it another chance. There were too many distractions in London.

Donna And there's me, I can get pregnant at the drop of a hat. Or a pair of knickers.

Michelle I don't know what it is.

Donna D'you think there might be something wrong? Have you been the doctor's?

Michelle I know it's not me.

Donna How?

Michelle Well, I . . . A few years ago . . .

Donna You got rid of one?

Michelle Yeah, it was before Robert. It was with that accountant, Gareth, I don't think you met him.

Donna The really boring one?

Michelle Yeah. It wasn't right and my career was the most important thing then.

Donna It's not now?

Michelle No, I really want this to work.

The doorbell goes.

Kathleen (*coming down the stairs*) I'll get it.

Michelle I want a family. That's all I want. It is good to be back. I've missed you, y'know.

Donna Oh give over.

Kirsty walks into the room on her mobile phone. She is dressed like she's going to the Oscars. She walks straight past Kathleen in the hall.

Kathleen Hello, Kirsty. (*Kathleen goes back down the hall to the kitchen.*)

Kirsty (*into phone*) Don't talk to me like that, y' dick . . . I've lost you now . . . (*She goes out by the french windows to get a signal.*) . . . Got y' . . . dick. . . . (*She goes out into the garden.*)

Michelle God, is that Kirsty?

Donna I hope so. Can you see now why I'm glad number two's a mute?

Michelle She hasn't half grown up. She's very glam. Is she going somewhere special?

Donna No, she dresses like a slut twenty-four-seven.

John comes down the stairs and into the living room.

John The view from that room at the top is out of this world. I reckon you'd have been able to see the ships being launched from up there.

Donna D'you remember you took us to a couple of them? (*to Michelle*) You were really scared of all the crowds.

Michelle Was I?

John There'd be thousands there on launch day. The whole of Birkenhead at the river, all together. Whole families and kids there, all fighting to get a good spec. Especially if it was a navy ship going out to fight at sea.

Michelle I remember them smashing the bottle.

John Eh, that moment when the ship starts off down the slipway, y' can't beat it. The crowd would go mad, like it was New Year's Eve.

Michelle Have something to eat, Dad.

John (*looking at the food*) D'you know what, I'm not hungry just yet.

Michelle No one's touched any of it.

Donna I can't look at those vine leaves.

John D'you know you've got a leak from the top bathroom dripping into the next one?

Michelle I do now.

John I've put a bucket under it. Where's there a toolbox?

Michelle Dad, sit down. Robert can fix it when he comes back.

John It'll get worse, all I've got to do is tighten the thingymebob.

Michelle There's a toolbox in the basement.

John Righty-o. (*John goes to the basement.*)

Michelle There's probably only a spanner in it. (*to Donna*) We normally just call someone, they charge you two hundred pounds and make it worse.

Donna Oh, London life, isn't it great.

Kirsty appears in the doorway, still on the phone.

Kirsty Go boil y' head . . . dick. (*She clicks her phone off.*) Hiya, Auntie Michelle.

Michelle Less of the auntie.

Kirsty This place is sound. I'm gonna have a house like this. Are y' gonna have a proper party? I could sort you out with a DJ. We could put the decks in the garden.

Michelle This is the party for the time being.

Kirsty Don't I get a drink?

Michelle What would you like? Coke, orange?

Kirsty Aren't I getting any champagne?

Michelle You drink? I'm sure you do.

Kirsty I've been drinking for years.

Michelle looks to Donna.

Donna You try and stop her doing anything.

Michelle goes into the kitchen. Kirsty goes to the hall door, to the pram.

Kirsty How's my beautiful Reinar?

Donna He's fasto.

Kirsty moves to pick him up.

Don't wake him up.

Kirsty I'll wake him up if I wannu. He's due for a feed soon.

Michelle comes back and hands a glass of champagne to Kirsty. Kirsty leaves Reinar alone.

Michelle You're breast-feeding?

Kirsty Is right.

Michelle I don't think you should be drinking.

Kirsty I'll only have a couple. He likes it anyway. I was drinking Bacardi the other night and he loved it. He was all giggly and cute.

Donna Are you for real? Just cut out the middleman and slip him a Bacardi Breezer.

Kirsty I might do that. I bet you he'd love it. They say y' kid gets a taste for whatever you had while you were pregnant. I should see if he likes prawn cocktail crisps, that's all I ate.

Donna (*looking outside*) Eddie, get down from that tree. If the cat wants to sit up there then leave it. (*Donna goes out into the garden.*)

Michelle I wouldn't have thought you'd have breast-fed, aren't bottles easier?

Kirsty I do a bit of both now. I've started using the pumper, so me mum gives him that or the bottle if I'm working or gonna be out all night. But I love it, you know, breastfeeding, I'm gonna miss it when I stop.

Michelle The bond between mother and son, that closeness?

Kirsty Naah, the size of me tits. They're massive at the moment. I'm not going back to two fried eggs. I might keep pumping them on the sly until I've saved up enough money to get them done.

Michelle You what?

Kirsty I'm gonna get me tits done.

Michelle Oh Kirsty, you don't want to do that.

Kirsty I know they look chunky now, but once he's off the tit they're gonna disappear again. I've got enough for me left one already. I've just got to save up for the right one, then I'll be made. You should get yours done, it'll make you much more attractive.

Michelle I don't think I need to. Anyway, I don't want two bags of plastic floating around inside my body, thank you very much. They don't even know what that stuff does to you.

Kirsty I reckon if they go funny and start leaking they'll have invented something else by then and I'll just get that put in. By then I'll be loaded so I'll be able to afford the best plastic surgeons.

Michelle How's that going to happen?

Kirsty I'm gonna be famous, aren't I?

Michelle And having plastic breasts is going to make you famous?

Kirsty No, but it'll help. You can't be famous and flat-chested. As me mate Dolores says, if I was doing page three I'd need signs saying 'front' and 'back'.

Michelle is speechless.

I know people don't believe me, but I am gonna be famous. That's what I want more than anything. I know I could be. I'd be really good at it.

Michelle At what, though? What are you going to do to become famous?

Kirsty I don't mind, I'll do whatever it takes. I could be a model, a pop star, on the telly, in films. I'm not bothered. Y' see people on the telly don't y' and y' think, I could do that. It'd be great. I wanna stay in hotels, travel on planes, buy designer clothes, not knock off stuff, and go to loads of parties. I want loads of money and loads of fans. I want people to know me. To want me. To want me autograph. To want to touch me. I wouldn't even mind having a stalker. Can you imagine what that must be like? That someone can't stop thinking about y' and that they follow y' everywhere. I'd be buzzing.

Michelle I think in reality being famous is pretty miserable most of the time.

Kirsty They all say that to put y' off, but how can it be? How can having anything y' want be miserable? Have you still got your flat in London?

Michelle No, we sold it to move here.

Kirsty Aah. Y' see, that's why I came along today. I had it all worked out. I reckoned I could go and live in your flat for a bit, become famous, then I'd have enough money to get a nanny. I'd bring Reinar down and we'd all live together in London. That's where it's all happening, isn't it? That's mad, that, you've moved away from there and come back 'ere. You've done it the wrong way round. It's a nice house and all that but there's no way you're gonna be famous now, are you? Up here.

Michelle I don't want to be famous.

Kirsty Yes, you do.

Michelle I couldn't think of anything worse.

Kirsty Everyone wants to be famous and anyone who says they don't is lying.

Michelle I think you'd find that most people wouldn't want it.

Kirsty Everyone I know, that's all they want. And it's the only way to get away from 'ere.

Michelle You don't want to stay around here?

Kirsty You got out, didn't y'?

Michelle Yeah, but things are changing. It's on the turn now.

Kirsty Naah, London's the place to be. What I'd really like is a place up 'ere and a place down there. I'm gonna do what Michael Owen did and buy me mum and me nan a street for them to live in. Eh, this one's nice. I could buy them houses either side of you.

Michelle But Michael Owen's got a real skill. He's a brilliant footballer. That's why he's famous and got all his money. Don't you want to be good at something? You know there's so many opportunities now, for your generation. Not like when me and your mum were your age. (*trying to inspire her*) Kirsty, you could do whatever you want.

Kirsty I know that. Once I get me tits done I'm on me way.

Donna (*coming back in*) If you want fame so much, go out and murder half of Birkenhead. You'll be on the front pages for weeks and everyone will know your name.

Kirsty You say that, but look at Nikki MacMahon. She's loving it.

Donna I don't think she is. (*explaining to Michelle*) The girl two doors along from us, her mum and her sisters were killed in a house fire.

Michelle nods, she's heard.

Kirsty She's been on the radio and the telly news. The *Echo* put her up in a hotel with a swimming pool for two nights and she could order anything she wanted from room service. Her room bill came to four hundred pounds.

Donna I'm sure it did.

Kirsty She even got asked for her autograph in the market and she's meant to be releasing a single, for charity. Dolores said she's gonna do 'Relight My Fire', but I think she's taking the piss.

Donna So if we were all barbecued you'd be over the moon, would y'?

John starts banging and hammering upstairs.

Kirsty No, but she always wanted to be famous and now she's got it. She says that fire was the best thing that's ever happened to her. The thing is with fame now, is you've just got to get people to notice y' and then once you're in there you can do whatever you want. I think if something did happen to me I'd get a lot more sympathy because I'm a single mother.

Reinar starts crying.

Oh, the little bastard.

Donna And he's off. Thanks, Dad.

Reinar continues to cry very loudly. The hammering stops.

Michelle He's very . . . loud, isn't he?

Donna Imagine that continually through the night.

Kirsty Go on, Mum, will you give him a bottle?

Michelle Ah, let me pick him up.

Donna No, she's gotta get used to looking after him. He doesn't even know who she is. Go and feed him, y' lazy cow.

Kirsty I could do with getting rid of some of this milk, me tits are killing me.

Donna I'm sure he's got a microphone and a couple of speakers in that pram.

Kirsty goes into the hall. Eddie comes in and stands next to Donna. He wants something.

Michelle How can she afford plastic surgery?

Donna She works in a bar in town.

Kirsty pushes the pram back and forward, bored. John starts hammering again. Reinar continues to cry. Eddie stares at Donna.

Donna What is it? (*to Michelle*) Have y' got a telly? He's bored.

Michelle It's through in the television room . . .

Donna Ooh, get you.

Michelle But we weren't going to have it on.

Donna It's like being in church. Can he just watch it for a bit? He won't have it on loud.

Michelle Okay, but I don't want everyone going through there and sitting round the telly.

Donna They won't. I'll make sure. (*to Eddie*) Come on.

Donna and Eddie go through to the television room.

Michelle Where's me mother?

Kathleen appears in the kitchen doorway wearing a brightly coloured apron, drying a plate with a tea towel.

Kathleen Just tidying up.

Michelle Mother, get out of there now. You're a guest, you're not going to do anything. You're just going to sit there and drink.

Kathleen I was enjoying meself.

Michelle (*in police speak, as if through a loud-hailer*) 'Put the tea towel down and move away from the sink.'

Kathleen comes through and sits down with a drink. The hammering stops. Kirsty picks up Reinar and walks up and down the hall with him.

The burgers. I haven't made the burgers.

Donna (*coming back in*) Couldn't you just go down to the Kwiky and buy forty frozen ones like everyone else? We're only going to set fire to them anyway.

Michelle I've got all the ingredients. They sound lovely. They're out of the Jamie Oliver.

Kathleen gets up to help.

Don't you move a muscle. Right. (*She finds the Jamie Oliver cook-book in one of the boxes and opens it.*) Botham burgers.

Michelle goes into the kitchen and collects the ingredients together. Reinar continues to cry.

Donna Kirsty, take him upstairs, I've had him screaming down me ear all night.

Kirsty (*to Reinar*) Isn't nanny a witch? Oh yes she is.

Kirsty goes upstairs with Reinar. The crying fades into the distance.

Robert (*coming back in*) They love us at Sainsbury's, I think we're keeping them in business. More drink. Brian's got the self-lighting no-smoke super coal.

John comes in through the kitchen door with a spanner in his hand, his hair soaking wet.

John Can I turn the water off for a minute?

Suddenly, very loudly, the groans and wonky music of a porn video can be heard from the television room. A man and a woman with American accents are reaching a climax.

Man's Voice Ah, ah, ah. Oh yeah, you like that?

Woman's Voice That's good. That's so good. Oh yeah, ride me, cowboy.

Everyone freezes.

Donna What the fuck's that?

Brian enters carrying the bag of coal.

Brian Bloody hell, what have I been missing?

Michelle and Robert run to the television room.

Man's Voice I'm gonna do it. I'm gonna do it.

Woman's Voice Go on, take it out, big boy.

Michelle Eddie, give me the remote. Where's the fuckin' remote?

Man's Voice Ow, ow, yeah, yeah.

Woman's Voice Oh yeah, all over my tits.

The sound stops sharply as the video is turned off.

Michelle Go inside, please, Eddie, that's a good boy.

Eddie comes through to the living room and sits down on the sofa.

(*to Robert*) What the fuck is that?

Michelle closes the door to the television room from inside. They all stand in the living room watching the door.

Brian (*to Eddie*) Well done, lad, that was class. Did y' see their faces?

Kathleen What was it?

John Kathleen!

Brian I wouldn't wanna be in that room with Michelle now.

John Come on, everyone, leave her be. Let's turn this water off. (*John goes into the kitchen.*)

Kathleen I'll . . . (*She goes into the kitchen.*)

Donna If we don't hear anything in a while someone should go in and resuscitate Robert.

Brian I wonder where he got it from.

Donna It could be Michelle's. No, it couldn't.

Brian (*going out to the barbecue*) Let's set fire to things.

Donna She'll come back out in a minute and make like nothing's happened.

Eddie goes into the garden.
Kathleen stands in the doorway wearing the apron, holding the Jamie Oliver book open in her hand.

Kathleen These burgers aren't going to make themselves.

Donna (*watching the door to the television room*) Well, they've got to come out of there sometime.

Kathleen (*coming out with the beef*) D'you think this beef is off? It's a funny colour. And smell it. (*She looks at the beef and sniffs it.*)

Donna It'll be fine as long as it's not British.

Kathleen It says it's organic, but . . . (*She looks out into the garden.*) Oh look, there's that cat. I know. (*She tears off a strip of beef.*) We'll do a little taste test. Here puss. (*She goes outside with the beef.*) Look what I've got.

Donna You can't do that. (*Donna watches.*) He's going for it. Oh, he likes that.

The door to the television room opens.

Ee are.

Donna picks up a magazine, like she's been reading it. It's upside down.
Michelle comes out with the video tape in her hand, the insides ripped out and wrapped round itself.

Michelle Let's have a tidy up, any more rubbish for the rubbish? (*She goes out the front door to the bin.*)

Kathleen (*coming back in*) The beef's fine.

Robert comes out of the television room, embarrassed but trying to put on a brave face. Donna sees the magazine's upside down and turns it the right way round.

Robert Let's get cooking.

Donna Yeah.

Brian It's lit!

Robert Man make fire.

Donna That sums you two up perfectly. It takes you hours to make a fire, you've just set civilisation back a million years.

Brian I'll keep an eye on it, Rob, we don't want it going out again. D'you wanna do us a top-up?

Robert grabs the champagne from the kitchen. Michelle comes back in. She's quiet and trying to keep busy.

Donna You've got him well trained.

Robert (*to Michelle*) Look, the barbecue's lit.

Michelle Three hours later. (*She goes into the kitchen and sees Kathleen making the burgers.*) Mother!

Kathleen I've nearly done them now.

Michelle Okay, okay, you do them, then.

Michelle comes back into the living room and moves round quickly, plumping up cushions and tidying up. Kirsty comes in. Robert sees Kirsty first. He stops and looks at her for a second. He clearly recognises her.

Kirsty He's asleep on Michelle's bed. (*Kirsty sees Robert.*) Hiya.

Donna Oh, this is Kirsty, me eldest. Robert, Michelle's fella.

Robert (*moving back towards the garden*) Hello.

Kirsty Don't I know you?

Robert No, I don't think so.

Michelle watches Robert, she can see he's uncomfortable.

Kirsty I've seen y' before.

Donna He's only been here a week. He must look like someone else.

Robert Yeah. (*Robert heads into the garden.*)

Kirsty I know . . .

Robert stops, caught at the door. His back to Kirsty.

Have you been on the telly?

Robert (*going back out*) That'll be it.

Kirsty Has he? Is he famous? What's he been on?

Donna University Challenge.

Kirsty What's that?

Donna Of course he hasn't. He's having you on.

Kirsty Oh, right.

Kirsty looks back out into the garden, watching Robert. She knows him. Michelle is intrigued.

Donna I think it's time for a wander.

Donna goes out and upstairs. Kathleen pops her head out of the kitchen with the recipe book in her hand.

Kathleen (*to Michelle*) It says herbs here, shall I leave them out?

Michelle No, I've bought fresh ones there.

Michelle goes through to the kitchen.

 Kirsty is left alone in the room. She takes out her mobile phone, scrolls to a number in her address book and calls it. Michelle and Kathleen move about in the kitchen in the background.

Kirsty Hiya, Chazza, it's Kirsty . . . Yeah, Miss Kirsty . . . I'm sound, I'm sound . . . I was just phoning to see if you're about tonight . . . I just wanted some 'tickets' for Cream . . . Quite a few, it'd be worth your while . . . I'd want a few of each . . . I could come to you . . . Er, yeah, you could deliver them 'ere . . . All right . . . I'm at number . . . twelve, Hilltop Road . . .D'you know where that is? . . . What are y' laughing at? . . . Y' jokin' . . . You're at number ten? . . . You haven't got a BMW, have y'? . . . Y' jokin' This is me auntie's house . . . I'll come round there. If that's all right . . . I've got the money with me . . . See y' in a minute . . . See y', Chazza.

She clicks the phone off. She takes a wad of cash out of her pocket and counts it out in her hand. Brian comes in from the garden.

Brian You won the lottery?

Kirsty What are y' doing? Eh? Creeping around, scaring the shit out of me?

Brian No. What are *you* doing? Counting out money, popping round to see Chazza. (*imitating her*) ''Bye, Chazza.'

Kirsty It's just the money for me boobs, that's all.

Brian And you're gonna give it to Chazza? He's doing the operation next door, is he? I wouldn't trust anyone called Chazza with y' precious knockers.

Kirsty Piss off, Brian.

Brian I know you're dealing.

Kirsty What?

Brian 'I want some tickets for Cream.' You could've been more imaginative than that. No one will be listening to your calls, anyway.

Kirsty So what if I sell a few pills and a bit of coke, it's only to me mates. It's only so I can save up for these. (*her breasts*) At least I'm getting off me arse and doing something with me life. I'm out of here.

Brian No, you're not.

Kirsty I am, y' can't stop me . . . You're . . .

Brian (*girly voice*) 'Not me dad.' (*Brian stands in front of her in the doorway.*)

Kirsty What d'you want, Bri?

Brian A wrap'll do. A little wrap of coke and we won't say anything.

Kirsty Get lost. I'll tell me mum.

Brian Go on, tell her. She'll hit the roof and there'll be no more looking after Reinar for you. Go on, I've got nothing to lose?

Michelle (*coming out of the kitchen with a box of candles*) Right, candles.

Kirsty Okay, then.

Michelle Let's have a look at this table, no doubt it's going to piss down. (*Michelle goes out into the garden.*)

Brian And I'll take that. (*He takes her phone out of Kirsty's hand.*) To make sure you come back. I know how your brain works, you'd just scarper.

Kirsty You can't take me phone.

Brian I just have. Now run along like a good little girl.

Kirsty (*storming out*) Dick.

Robert (*coming in*) I'm keeping out of her way.

Brian Rob, will it be all right if we watch *Millionaire* later?

Robert I don't think Michelle will want it on.

Brian She won't mind. Eh, have y' seen those *Millionaire* machines they have in pubs, they've got one in the Duke. You never win, though, the time goes too fast. It's a right swizz.

Robert I've got it on the Playstation.

Brian You haven't. Go on then.

Robert Michelle'll go mad. She doesn't even know I've still got the Playstation. She made me throw it out, but I smuggled it up here.

Michelle comes back in, Eddie follows her.

Not just now. (*for Michelle's benefit*) Looks like we could put some food on soon.

Robert and Brian both sidle back outside.

Michelle Come on, let's go inside. Why don't we sit down for a second? We could have a nice chat.

Michelle sits down on the sofa. Eddie doesn't move.

Come on, I don't bite.

Eddie walks over and sits next to Michelle. He looks at her.

We haven't had a chance to get to know each other. And I think we should. I'm going to be living here for good now, so if you ever want to talk . . . or want to have some space. If your mum and dad are doing your head in, you can always come here. Whenever you want. (*Pause.*) Now this not speaking. I'm sure you think it's easier and that your mum and dad don't care, but they do, you know. It would make them so happy if you started speaking again. And you could tell her when you were unhappy or angry or sad.

Pause. No response. He just looks at her.

I won't tell anyone else, you could just speak to me, this can be our secret.

He doesn't respond. She has an idea.

I know. Let's put some music on. (*She jumps up and roots through a box of CDs.*) Ee are Classic Hits, Mozart, Mozart. Here we are. (*She puts the CD on.*) Number five. (*The music starts. She turns the volume up loud. She sits back down.*) Isn't that nice? You still don't want to say anything? You don't trust me, do you? Why should you? I know what we'll do, we'll play a game. Do you want to play a game?

He smiles.

Maybe? A trust game. You'll like it, it'll be a laugh. Are you up for this? Oh go on. What we need is something for you to stand on. (*She grabs two boxes of books and puts them on top of each other – to create a high platform next to the sofa.*) Right, climb up here.

He doesn't move.

I know you can do this. Come on.

Eddie gets up, she takes his hand and he climbs up using the sofa like stairs and then onto the boxes. Michelle stands behind him and holds her arms out to catch him.

67

Now what you do is, you fall backwards and I'm going to catch you. Yeah, I know it's scary but you can do it. It's all about trust. You've got to trust me. Close your eyes it's even better. Just fall, fall back now.

John (*coming in from the kitchen*) Water's back on.

Donna (*coming in from upstairs*) What the fuck's going on here?

Eddie loses his balance, falls forward and disappears behind the sofa with a crash.

Michelle Eddie!

Donna Oh, my God.

Kathleen appears in the kitchen door. Robert and Brian come in from outside. Donna rushes to pick Eddie up. He stands up slightly dazed, half-holding his head. The music still plays loud.

Michelle Is he all right?

Donna Have you hurt yourself? Have you banged your head? Come and sit down. Fuckin' hell, I don't believe this. (*She sits him down on the sofa.*)

Michelle I'm so sorry.

Donna What were you doing? What were you playing at? Will someone turn that fuckin' awful music off.

Robert turns the music off.

Michelle It's a trust game, we did it at work.

Donna He's seven, he's not on a management training scheme.

Michelle I thought if he trusted me he might start talking again.

Donna Well, he's not going to speak now, is he? That bump has probably knocked every last word out of his body. What a bloody stupid idea. Look at him, he's in shock.

Robert Should I call an ambulance?

John He looks all right. Are you all right, son?

Kathleen Does anything hurt?

Eddie shakes his head.

Brian There's nothing wrong with him.

Donna (*to Michelle*) He could've rolled into the barbecue or impaled himself on something. Have you got no common sense? I don't believe you sometimes.

John Eh, Donna, I think that's enough.

Kathleen He's fine.

Reinar starts crying.

Donna Oh great. Where's Kirsty?

Brian She's just popped out.

Michelle starts crying.

Donna Oh my God. That's all we need.

Donna (*to Eddie*) You okay?

Eddie nods.

Rescued by Reinar. (*Donna goes out and upstairs.*)

Michelle I just thought . . . It just seemed so . . . Oh, what have I done? Everything I try to do goes wrong. It's all a disaster.

Robert moves over towards her. She reaches out to John, who is standing next to her.

Michelle Oh, Dad, what am I doing? (*She hugs John and starts to cry.*)

John Don't worry. Don't worry yourself, girlie.

Kathleen (*to Eddie*) You come with me.

She takes Eddie by the hand and leads him out into the garden.

Brian (*quiet, to Robert*) Let's get *Millionaire* on.

Robert and Brian go into the television room. Michelle and John are left alone.

Michelle What was I doing? Donna's right, it was a stupid idea in the first place.

John Eh, no. You meant to do the right thing.

Michelle I always get everything wrong. I mean well but I always get it wrong. (*She starts to sob.*) Oh, Dad, what am I doing?

John Come on, 'Chelle, it was a little accident, no one's hurt, there's no need to get so upset. It's nothing, don't cry.

Michelle I can't do anything right. Everything goes wrong. Everything. Why don't I stop and think? Why don't I think what's going to happen? Oh, Dad, what am I going to do? What am I going to do? I'm sorry. I'm so sorry.

John You've got nothing to be sorry for. Eddie's fine. You're going to stop crying and blow your nose. It'll be all right, shush. Shush now.

He takes a cotton hankie out of his pocket. It has a J stitched into the corner. He hands it to her. She looks at it.

Michelle I bought you this.

John I know.

Michelle About twenty years ago!

John Just blow your nose.

She blows her nose and wipes her eyes.

Michelle Look at the state of me now.

John Where did that all come from?

Michelle I don't know. Who can I blame? I think it was Robert's fault.

John Yeah, you're right.

Michelle It's good to be back.

John And not a moment too soon.

Michelle D'you mean that?

John Of course I do. It hasn't been the same without you 'ere. It was a sad day the day you left. I've had to put up with your mother and Donna ganging up on me. But we're all back together now. And everything's sorted itself out. You couldn't have come at a better time. You know, even though I'm getting me old job back, I had to get out of that car park because I thought, I can't have my Michelle seeing me working here, doing this.

She starts to cry again.

John Oh, 'Chelle, 'Chelle. What are y' crying at now? That was meant to make y' feel better. Come on.

Pause.

I haven't seen y' cry like this since y' cat got run over by the milkman.

Michelle (*laughing through the tears*) Seefor.

John That was always a stupid name. C for cat. It was a right dozy thing getting run over by a milkfloat doing ten miles an hour.

Michelle wipes her eyes.

Or when we took you to London when you first started college.

Michelle Oh God, that first night away from home was horrible. I cried all night. Am I always crying? I'm a right whinger, aren't I?

John What's this all about?

Michelle It's coming back here. Everything. What have I been doing? What am I doing now?

John You're back, that's all that matters. Eh, but you've got to promise me you won't run off again.

Michelle I promise. I'm staying. I'm not going anywhere. This is my home now.

John My little 'Chelle. Little Sea-Shell.

Michelle *and* **John** 'Chelle sells sea-shells on the sea shore.

They both smile. Pause.

John Can I let everyone back in now?

Michelle Have I just made a real tit of myself?

John You're allowed.

Michelle Ee are. (*She passes him the handkerchief.*)

John Keep it.

John gets up and gives her a kiss.

I wish you hadn't had all your hair cut off. Right, everyone, show's over.

The doorbell goes. Michelle gets up.

Michelle I'm going to clean myself up. Ta, Dad.

Robert comes out of the television room to get the door. He stops for a second to see Michelle.

Brian Don't leave me, Rob, I'm on eight thousand 'ere and I've got no lifelines left.

Michelle Is that that fuckin' Playstation? I give up.

Michelle goes upstairs. Robert goes to get the door. John goes to the kitchen to get a top-up. Kirsty comes into the living room.

Kirsty (*to Robert*) I know where I've seen you.

Robert (*going out to the barbecue*) You're thinking of someone else.

Brian (*coming out of the television room*) Aah, I've just lost seven grand. Who the fuck's Clement Attlee?

John For crying out loud, don't say you haven't heard of him. Come on, let's win a million. I feel lucky.

John goes into the television room.

Kirsty You won't be getting any again.

She passes him a small folded wrap of coke.

Brian It'd better not be cut with a load of crap.

Robert (*coming in*) Nearly time to put the food on.

Kirsty I've got some phone calls to make. A drink first. (*She walks past Robert towards the kitchen.*) Does Michelle know you were at a lap-dancing club last night?

73

She walks into the kitchen. Robert is clearly rattled.

Brian Eh, Rob, are you a fan of the Peruvian nose flute?

Robert Is that that aztecy music? Yeah, it's good, I think I've heard some of it. I like the gypsy kings.

Brian Naah, I mean Prince Charles is in the building. (*Brian sniffs.*)

Robert I don't know what you're talking about.

Brian (*showing him the wrap*) D'you wanna line?

Robert Oh. No, no. I couldn't, I shouldn't. I'd love to but . . . No.

Brian I won't tell if you don't.

Robert Doesn't Donna mind?

Brian She does now. She didn't used to, but she can't be bothered with it now. We'd put the kids to bed, do a few lines, talk crap, have a shag and then they'd be up again. I'd just go to bed but she'd be off to work, she was done in.

Kirsty comes out of the kitchen with a drink, looks over to Robert. He wants to get away.

Robert Go on then.

Robert and Brian go into the hall. Kirsty punches a number into her phone and goes outside.

(*whispering, very seriously*) We'll go down to the basement, Michelle's upstairs.

Robert stalls for a minute. He glances up the stairs where Michelle is, then rushes off to the basement.

John (*from the television room*) Yes!

Michelle and Donna come down the stairs and into the living room.

Donna He's back asleep for ten minutes.

Michelle Right, this is meant to be a party. Why don't we play some games, while we wait for the food? And then we'll play some more after we've eaten.

Donna (*mock over-excitement*) Let's skip the food and play games all night.

Michelle It'll be a laugh. Where is everyone? It's all getting dispersed, we should all be in the same room.

Donna Maybe they're already playing hide-and-seek.

Michelle Sit down, I'll get everyone together.

Donna sits down. She prods the food but doesn't eat it.

Donna Why do you always go for posh blokes? Even as a kid you wouldn't have anything to do with the scallies off the estate.

Michelle I don't, do I?

Donna Yeah, you think you're one of them, don't y'?

Michelle No, it's just the people you meet, isn't it? And I know Robert seems different to us, but he's not at all. He's got that confidence posh people have, but I think that's great. I wish I had more of it, believed in myself more. He was brought up being told he could be whatever he wanted. Not like us.

Donna Yeah, but for him it's probably true.

Michelle Well, yeah, I know I'm sure he could have some high-powered job raking it in but he's not interested in ambition or money. He'd much rather be creative. That's really what I was first attracted to.

Robert and Brian enter through the kitchen door. They are both smoking. Robert really drags on his cigarette.

Michelle Two more. We're going to play a game.

Robert (*not keen*) It's that time already?

Michelle Robert, you're smoking.

Robert Well spotted. I just felt like one. You know, when you just feel like one. I haven't had a cigarette for ages, well I had one just before this one but apart from that . . .

Brian (*to Robert*) Shall we make a move? Let's just see how J's getting on. (*Brian goes into the television room.*)

Robert Won't be long.

Michelle What?

Robert Brian's taking me into town for a drink. He's going to show me the sights of Birkenhead. That should take about five minutes.

He laughs, Michelle is not amused.

Michelle There's plenty of drink here.

Robert Change of scene. Fresh air. Barbecue's ready. By the time we get back all the food'll be ready. My work is done.

Michelle What about me?

Robert You can come too if you want.

Michelle Do you really want to go for a drink with Brian?

Robert You can have some quality time with your family. I thought you'd like that.

Michelle (*looking at him*) Are you feeling all right?

Brian comes out of the television room.

Brian He's on a sixty-four thousand there and he's only used ask the audience. (*to Michelle*) Don't worry, 'Chelle, I'll look after him.

Robert You don't mind, do you?

Michelle (*annoyed*) Why would I mind? Enjoy yourselves.

Brian Be half an hour tops.

Michelle Be as long as you want.

Robert and Brian go out.

Michelle We can still play.

Donna No, you're right, Robert is different, he's just as useless as Brian.

Michelle I'll get me mum and dad. What shall we play?

Donna Can't we just relax, sit, drink?

John comes out of the television room.

John (*reading the question*) What was the name of the snail in the children's television series *The Magic Roundabout*?

Donna *and* **Michelle** (*simultaneously*) Brian!

John Ta, girls. It's a hundred and twenty-five thousand.

Donna Let's have a look. (*to Michelle*) You get everyone together, call me when you're ready.

John and Donna go into the television room. Michelle is left alone. She picks at the food, taking a bite of a stuffed vine leaf. It's not very nice, but she swallows it down. A cheer from John and Donna. Michelle goes to the doors to the garden.

Michelle Would you like to play a game, Mum?

Kathleen (*standing in the doorway*) Ooh, yeah. How about *Give Us a Clue*? I love *Give Us a Clue*.

Michelle Okay, we can play that first.

Kathleen comes in followed by Eddie. Donna comes through.

Donna (*to Kathleen*) Mum, we're on quarter of a million, it's a question about the Pope. I'm sure you'll know it.

Kathleen Save me a seat, Michelle.

Donna and Kathleen all go into the television room. Michelle is left with Eddie.

Michelle I suppose you don't want to play another game with me.

Eddie looks at her and walks into the kitchen.

Michelle Oh, this is great.

John (*from the television room*) Yes!

Michelle looks out into the garden and spots Kirsty heading towards the house.

Michelle Kirsty?

Kirsty enters from the garden on her phone.

Kirsty Not now (*into phone*) . . . You're outside . . . Yes, that 'big fuck-off house' is me auntie's . . . Yeah, I've got 'em . . . If you buy ten I'll give y' one free . . .

And she's gone out to the front door.
Michelle walks into the hall and stands at the door to the television room.

Michelle Are you all going to sit in here? It's meant to be a party . . .

Donna, John and Kathleen all shush her.

John You might know this one, 'Chelle.

Michelle stays watching.
Eddie enters the living room from the kitchen door. The room is empty. He looks out of the doors into the garden. He stops still. He's watching something on the ground outside the doors. It's the cat. A dark cloud passes over the garden. Eddie bends down and rubs his fingers together to attract the cat to him. He moves slowly forward.

Eddie (*a whisper*) Here puss, pss, pss, pss. Here puss.

A friendly miaow from the cat. He slowly moves forward and then quickly as he picks it up just outside the door. Out of sight.

Gotcha.

The cat miaows again. The cat lets out a yelp and another. Then a scream like it's in a fight. Then the loud crack of its neck being snapped. Eddie throws the cat across the garden. The rustle as it lands in a bush. Eddie comes back in and brushes fur off his hands like a workman who's just completed a difficult job. He stands still silently in the middle of the room and smiles.
A cheer from the television room. Michelle comes back into the living room. She sees Eddie and jumps, not expecting him to be there.

Michelle Eddie! You gave me the fright of my life.

Eddie turns, looks at Michelle and walks out into the television room.

Michelle stands still in the middle of the empty room. She has a swig of her drink.

Great party, this is. Right. Burgers.

She goes into the kitchen and comes through with the burgers. She starts putting them on the barbecue.
A loud cheer goes up from the television room.
John comes rushing out into the living room, followed by the others.

John I've just won a million. I'm a millionaire. This feels great.

Donna That was superb.

Kathleen Well done, John. I would never have got that. I thought Orinoco was a Womble, not a river.

John I really feel like I've won it. This is fantastic.

John takes Michelle by the arms and dances round the room with her.

Donna Now this is a reason to drink champagne. Let's get another one open.

Kathleen gets the glasses ready. Donna cracks open a bottle of champagne. Eddie watches from the hall. John dances round the room with an awkward Michelle, holding her tight.

End of Act One.

Act Two

*Michelle, Kathleen, Donna and Kirsty sit round on the
sofa with pieces of paper in front of them. Wild Swans
by Jung Chang is on the coffee table. The food has been
cleared away. They are playing a game. Kirsty is on the
phone. It is later, the sun is starting to set.*

Michelle Are we all done?

Kirsty (*into phone*) It's the next right after that.

Kathleen I can't think what to put.

Donna Just write anything, it doesn't matter.

Michelle Take your time, Mother, we want to play it
properly.

Kirsty I've done mine.

Donna I thought it was a game. Y'know, fun.

Michelle It is, but it's more fun if we play it properly
and really try and be creative.

Donna And you say you've had a laugh playing this?

Michelle It's great. There's nights where my stomach
hurts from laughing so much.

Donna We've got that to look forward to.

Kathleen But aren't you gonna know what the first line
is because it's your book.

Donna Yeah, you'll have read it.

Kirsty But didn't you write down the real one anyway?

Kathleen I don't understand now.

Kirsty *(into phone)* Straight on and it's number twelve, Riverview. See y' in a minute. *(She clicks off her phone.)*

Michelle Right, I've written down what I think it could be. A guess, and I've put that in. And *then* I wrote the real first line and put that in. *After* I'd written mine.

Kirsty I think she's cheating.

Michelle I'm not, what would be the point of cheating?

Donna So you'd win. You always want to win.

Kathleen I don't know if it's fair that you picked your own book.

Michelle I picked one at random and I read it years ago, I can't remember. Anyway it's not about getting it exactly right, but guessing how it *could* be written, making it up.

A small explosion comes from the television room. Eddie's playing a computer game.

Kathleen You could have picked a better book.

Donna We're not gonna have heard of any of them. They're all posh books.

Kathleen We should pick ones that have been on the telly.

Michelle That sort of defeats the object.

The doorbell goes. Kirsty gets up and goes out.

Kathleen You're very popular today, aren't you?

Michelle How come she's selling tickets for a nightclub?

Donna Don't ask me.

Michelle Are y' sure me dad doesn't want to play?

Donna (*looking out into the garden*) I think he made the right choice. He's watching the barbecue. Well, with his eyes closed, horizontal in that deckchair.

Machine-gun fire and screams from the television room.

Michelle Is he all right in there?

Donna Yeah. You okay, love?

No reply.

You should see him, he's great, y'know. The speed he can work those controls. He can kill a whole troop of mutant zombies just like that. I had a go the other week and they'd ripped me apart within seconds.

Michelle I can't stand the Playstation. Once Robert's on it, that's it for the next two days. You can't communicate with him.

More explosions and screams.

Donna (*shouting through*) Will you turn that down a bit? It feels like we're in Vietnam.

Pause. They're waiting for Kathleen.

Kathleen I'm nearly there.

Michelle Do you know who the first person I saw when I got back was? Sharon Summers from school.

Donna Lucky you.

Michelle Oh God, she looked rough. She was walking through town with this pram surrounded by about forty kids.

Donna She's got more kids than teeth.

Kathleen I can't even remember what the book was about now.

Michelle Shall I read the bit on the back out again?

Donna No, no. It's about some Chinese woman, that's all you need to know.

Pause.

Donna Isn't it peaceful without the men about? I could get used to this. Wouldn't life be much simpler if they weren't 'ere. It's them that create all the trouble. All men have ever done is fuck things up.

Kathleen Donna.

Donna Well that's what I think.

Michelle I like men. I think there's a lot to be said for them.

Donna Like what?

Michelle Well . . .

Kirsty comes back in.

Kathleen Don't your friends want to come in?

Kirsty Naah. Are we nearly done yet?

Donna Go through history, it's men that have fucked things up. Can you think of any women that have made the world worse?

Kathleen Mrs Thatcher.

Donna Yeah, but she was a man, wasn't she? Well, she behaved like a man.

Kirsty Myra Hindley.

Michelle How d'you know about her?

Kirsty We did about her at school. I did a project on serial killers. Got an A.

Kathleen Yeah, Myra Hindley, that's a good one.

Michelle Is this a new game?

Kirsty It's better than yours.

Donna Yeah, but she was under the spell of a man, wasn't she?

Kathleen You have to have men to father your children.

Donna Once they've done the deed, there's no other use for them. Although some of them can't even do that. (*She looks to Michelle.*)

Kirsty I've never met me dad and look at me, I'm fine. Little Reinar's never going to meet his dad. He doesn't need him. He doesn't even know he's got a kid.

Kathleen But you've got to have a man to make the baby in the first place. You can't ever get away from that.

Michelle I know two women in London who've both had kids on their own. They just went to a clinic, got inseminated by an anonymous donor, went off and had a baby. There was never any father in the story and there isn't going to be.

Kathleen Can you do that? You don't have to be with someone?

Michelle As long as you've got the money you can do whatever you want.

Kathleen has thought of a line, she writes it down.

Donna Give it a couple of years and they'll be making babies on computers and you won't need them to even wank into a Petri dish. You won't be working at Cadbury's, you'll be working down the sprog factory.

Kirsty It'd be nice if y' could pick what type y' wanted. I'd like a black one. They're cuter.

Donna Y' know, I think if y' brought y' kids up with no men in their lives, just surrounded by a group of women, you'd have clever, hard-working kids. All this fighting and scrapping would go out the window.

Michelle The conversations would be better.

Donna Even the sex gets boring after a bit.

Michelle Mmm.

Kathleen I don't know what I'd do without y' dad.

Donna Ah, isn't me mum old-fashioned? Me dad's a different generation, isn't he? When they knew what they were doing and had a purpose. All I think about is life without Brian. (*to Michelle*) Are you gonna ditch Robert if he doesn't come up with the goods?

Michelle Can we get back to the game?

Donna Do we have to?

Kathleen I've done mine now.

Kathleen places her piece of paper in a pile with everyone else's.

Michelle I'll just read out the back bit again.

Donna Just get on with it.

Michelle It gives you a little reminder. So right, the first quote was – (*She reads.*) 'Of all the personal histories to have emerged out of China's twentieth-century nightmare, *Wild Swans* is the most deeply thoughtful and the most heartrending I've read. It moves, in part, like a ghastly oriental fairytale, but the authority and the reticent passion with which Jung Chang speaks her memories – and those of others – is unmistakable.' And there's . . .

86

Donna That's enough. We've already heard them all.

Michelle So now we have to vote on which one we think is the real one. Give them a little mix. (*She shuffles them and picks one out.*) Right. (*reading*) 'Ching Chang worked in a nightclub, she could fire ping-pong balls across the room at fifty miles an hour.' Are they all going to be like this?

Donna (*to Kirsty*) That's yours, isn't it?

Kathleen (*to Donna*) D'you think so? I thought it was –

Michelle No, no, we don't guess who wrote it. We guess if it's the real one.

Kathleen But I liked trying to work out whose it was.

Michelle But that's not how you play it.

Donna You see, we're not playing it to enjoy ourselves, we're playing it to be right. The most important thing is that we play it correctly.

Michelle Don't be like that.

Kathleen I liked guessing.

Michelle Well, why don't we play it my way first and see if we like it and then we could play it your way.

Kathleen Okay.

Michelle (*picking up another piece of paper*) So this one.

Kirsty D'you get to read them all out?

Michelle Yeah . . . That's just the way you play it. (*She reads.*) 'Sweet and sour pork twice with extra chips, said Po Lo to the man behind the counter at the Golden Dragon.'

They all look between each other. Nodding, winking and trying not to laugh. They know it's Kathleen's but they think they're being really subtle.

Michelle Do we think that's the real one?

Kathleen (*trying to be mysterious*) It could be, couldn't it?

Donna Oh yeah. That sounded like that Jung Chang.

Michelle What do you think, Kirsty?

Kirsty Let's just get on with it. I'm going out soon.

Michelle (*reads very proudly, it's hers*) 'This is the history of China seen through the eyes of three women, my mother, my grandmother and myself.'

Kirsty Next.

Donna I wonder whose it is?

Kathleen I feel like a Slippery Nipple.

Michelle You what?

Donna Let's not start on them, Mother.

Kathleen (*going to the kitchen*) It'll give us a little pep-up while we wait for the food. Have y' got Bailey's and sambuca?

Michelle There's a bottle of Bailey's there.

Kathleen Good. I'll use that tequila instead. Go on, I can still hear.

Michelle Right. (*She reads.*) 'At the age of fifteen my grandmother became the concubine of a warlord general, the police chief of a tenuous national government of China.'

Donna Boring. Whose is that?

Kathleen No, didn't like that one.

Kathleen comes in with a tray with four small shot glasses and the bottle of Bailey's and tequila.

Four Slippery Nipples coming up. This'll wake us up.

Michelle And here's the last one. (*She reads Donna's out.*) The day I had my feet bound I knew that the life of a woman in China was very different to that of a man's.'

Kathleen Ooh, that's the one.

Kathleen pours out four drinks. Half tequila topped up with Bailey's.

Michelle I don't think I want one.

Kathleen Just try it.

Michelle So which one do we think is the winner, the real one?

Kathleen The last one.

Kirsty Yeah, the last one.

Donna Fine by me.

Michelle Shall I read them all again?

Kirsty No, whose was it?

Donna It was mine.

Kathleen Well done. That was good, that.

Michelle Mmm, yeah.

Kathleen (*to Donna*) When you were captain of the netball team, you always won, didn't y'?

Michelle I never even got picked.

Kathleen But you were good at your schoolwork.

Donna Does that mean it's my go?

Michelle Yeah, you can go and pick a book. We don't have to play. It's probably the wrong game to play here.

Donna I quite enjoyed that.

Kathleen So did I.

Donna Okay, okay. Let's have a look.

She gets up and has a look through the boxes of books. Kathleen finishes pouring out the drinks.

Michelle Do we want to know which was the real one?

Kirsty Naah.

Kathleen Pick something we've heard of.

Donna There's no chance of that 'ere.

Kathleen Right, everyone. (*She passes them round.*) Knock 'em back. There's a prize for who finishes first.

Donna (*to Michelle*) I'm sure you can win at this.

Kathleen Go.

They all knock them back. Michelle finishes hers first.

Michelle Done.

Kirsty That's nice.

Donna Eeh.

Kathleen I love the kick. It works well with tequila.

Michelle Me mouth's gone numb. What do I get?

Kathleen The prize is . . . another Slippery Nipple.

Michelle I think I'll pass.

Kathleen No, no, you've got to have your prize.

Kathleen pours out another drink for Michelle and passes it to her.

Kathleen You can sip this one if you want.

Michelle (*looks at the drink in her hand*) Fuck it.

Michelle knocks it back in one.

Kathleen Michelle!

The doorbell rings. Kirsty goes to get up.

Michelle I'll get it.

Michelle gets up. The doorbell goes again.

(*going out*) Okay, okay. I'm coming.

Donna (*looking through the boxes of books*) Bloody hell, does she just go for things with stupid names? (*She picks out a book.*) *How to Get What You Want and Want What You Have.* What the fuck does that mean?

Michelle Oh my God, what happened? Oh, Robert.

Robert steps into the living room, escorted by Michelle. He has a bloody nose and a gash above his eye. There is blood all over his shirt and beer up one leg of his trousers. Brian follows without a scratch on him.

Donna Oh, 'ere we go. What the fuck have you been up to?

Kathleen Oh, Robert, you poor love.

Kirsty Welcome to Birkenhead.

Brian Y' should have seen it, it was like the Alamo.

Michelle What happened?

Brian Have you booked some entertainment? There's two girls outside who look like a couple of strippers.

Kirsty They'll be for me.

Brian Of course they are.

Kirsty (*sarcastic*) Thanks, Brian. (*rushing out*) Aah, I'm gonna miss what happened.

Kathleen Come and sit down. Look at the state of y'. And that lovely shirt, make sure you get some Vanish on that before you wash it. Let me get you cleaned up. Have y' got a first-aid box, cotton wool, anything?

Robert There's that first-aid kit I nicked from work.

Michelle You said to me they were throwing it out.

Kathleen It doesn't matter. Where is it?

Robert points through to the front room next door.

Michelle It'll be in amongst boxes and unpacked stuff.

Kathleen (*going out*) I'll find it.

Michelle What happened?

Donna (*to Brian*) You seem to have come out of it in one piece.

Brian I was lucky.

Michelle Should we call an ambulance?

Brian No, it's just a drop of blood. No harm done.

Michelle Will somebody tell me what happened?

Robert I really don't know.

Brian We just got into a fight, nothing major. I didn't even finish me pint.

Robert It could've all been avoided, there was no need for any of it.

Brian I saved your arse in there, mate.

Michelle Should I call the police?

Robert You were helping me?

Brian If I'd have just left you there you'd have more than a bit of blood down y' shirt.

Donna What actually happened, Bri?

Brian We'd gone to Yates', it was the first place we went. We were having a pint, weren't we. It was busy, like, but not too bad. There were these two lads behind us tanked up, they must've been drinking all day. Me and him are minding our own business. I go to the bog for a – (*He gestures towards his nose, then thinks better and tries to cover it.*) – for a squirt.

Donna Too much detail, get on with it.

Brian Anyway, I come back from the bog and there's Robert with half his pint on the floor and the other half down the front of his kecks. And there's this ginger short-arse staring at Robert like he's just shot his grandma.

Michelle You can't leave him for a minute.

Robert He'd walked into me, knocked my drink out of my hand and it'd gone everywhere.

Brian I could see this lad was about to kick off, so I got straight in there. (*Pause.*) And I fucked him. I just went bam and he fell back and he comes at me again and I just gave him two more, bam, bam, and he was on the floor. He wasn't getting up after that.

Robert There was no need for any of it. We could have just sat down and sorted it all out.

Brian He was a dickhead, he didn't give a toss what you were gonna say. If you weren't there it would've been someone else. I bet y' he knocked the drink over on purpose. It was either he gets fucked or you get fucked. That's it. I've had enough run-ins to know when someone's gonna kick off. I don't wanna be scrapping in the street but if you don't show them that y' can stand up for yourself, then you're done.

Robert If something did happen, we could have just called the police.

Brian I'll leave you next time. I'll let you deal with it.

Kathleen comes in with a first-aid box in the shape of the Millennium Dome.

Kathleen The stuff you've got in there. Did someone work at the Millennium Dome?

Michelle He helped out in the marketing department for a couple of months, as a favour.

Kathleen Let's have a look at y'. (*She opens it and cleans him up with the contents.*) There's some good quality stuff in 'ere.

Donna Hang on a mo'. What else happened? Why does Robert 'ere look like he went three rounds with Mike Tyson if it was you that was doing the punching?

Brian When I hit this lad, he shit a brick, didn't he? I've never seen anyone run so fast. Into a wall.

Michelle You ran into a wall?

Robert Yes.

Donna A wall did this?

Donna and Michelle look at each other. They try their best to keep their laughter in.

94

Robert Oh, it's funny now, is it?

Michelle Oh, come on, I thought you'd been savaged but you just banged your head. You could've done that here.

Kathleen cleans up the cut on his head.

Robert (*it stings*) Ah!

Kathleen It was a dirty wall. It looks like you've got a broken nose.

Robert Rugby at school.

Donna There's people in work who won't go down town any more. There's nutters who go down there just to get pissed and look for a fight. Although, what else have they got to do?

Michelle It's terrible.

Brian (*to Michelle*) Where've you been living? I thought you'd been living in London, not Toytown.

Michelle There's plenty of that sort of stuff going on in London. There was a woman in our road in Clapham who answered the door one day and this bloke cut her throat, just like that. Apparently he thought she was a drug-dealer's girlfriend. She was the cleaner.

Brian (*looking at the barbecue*) It looks like we got back in time for the food to be done.

Kathleen has finished repairing Robert.

Kathleen (*to Robert*) You'll live.

Donna (*going to the barbecue, to John*) Oi, Grandad, it's time you got up.

Kathleen Y' don't go to someone else's house to have a kip.

John I wasn't asleep.

Donna They're just right. Burgers and batches all round?

John (*coming in*) Y' see I've been keeping an eye on them for y'.

Donna Mum?

Kathleen Go on, I'll have a try of one of me home-made burgers. Make sure it's well done, cooked through.

> *Donna gets together burgers, buns and salad on a plate.*

John Stick one on a plate for me.

Kirsty (*coming back in*) I'll have one.

John (*about Robert*) What happened 'ere?

Michelle (*half-laughing*) He ran into a wall.

Robert Oh yeah, it's hilarious.

John (*sitting down*) I'm saying nothing.

Robert I'll go and get myself cleaned up.

> *Robert goes upstairs.*

Michelle Why don't we go and sit in the garden?

Brian (*to Michelle*) Oh, yeah. I bumped into Speedy in town, who I used to work with in Cadbury's, and he said that he hadn't heard of you working there or any new managers starting. And he's quite high up now.

Michelle Really . . .

> *Donna gives a burger each to Kathleen and Kirsty. John is next in line.*

Donna Ee are. Kirsty. (*all posh*) And a serviette each.

John Get us a big one, Don, I'm starving.

Donna goes back out to the barbecue.

Kathleen That'll be 'cause it's top secret, won't it.

Michelle (*plucking up the courage*) Well, actually, I should tell you . . .

Kathleen and Kirsty both take a bite. Donna screams from the garden. She comes running back in.

Donna Fuckin' hell. Jesus fuckin' Christ. I don't believe it, they're all after me. The whole spirit world is against me.

Brian What is it now?

Donna It's Welcome. Tiddles, he's dead. He was lying in the bush and I went to stroke him and his head just flopped to one side, his eyes staring at me.

Michelle Are you sure?

Donna Look at him, he's a stiff. Maybe he's having a laugh, holding his breath.

Michelle (*going out to look*) Oh, what's happened to him?

Kathleen spits the burger in her mouth out onto her serviette.

Donna Oh God, Mother, what's wrong with y'? Are they getting to you? What's going on?

Kathleen (*finishes spitting it out*) Sorry about that. I gave it some of that beef, didn't I?

Michelle (*coming back in*) He's dead all right. The poor thing.

Kirsty goes to take another bite, she's not been listening. Kathleen snatches the burger out of her hand.

Kathleen The beef's off.

Michelle It can't be, I only bought it yesterday. It was really expensive. It was organic.

Kirsty It tasted nice.

Kathleen Have you swallowed any?

Kirsty (*getting up and going the toilet*) I'll make meself sick.

Kathleen Oh, Kirsty.

Kirsty I've done it before, how else d'you think I've got a figure like this?

John We can't have any burgers?

Donna It's not the burgers, it's Mrs Winstanley.

Brian 'Ere we go.

Donna No, I knew it, I knew there was a presence 'ere that wasn't at rest. It's definitely her, she's not happy about something.

Brian Maybe it's all the scallies that have taken over her house.

John So this is how ghosts let you know they're about these days, murder a moggy.

Kathleen Why would she kill a cat?

Donna What else is she going to do? Eddie! Is he okay?

She turns round and he's standing in the doorway watching.

There you are, you're alright. Reinar. I'm gonna go and check on Reinar. (*She moves to go, then stops.*) Oh, he'll be fine. I don't want to wake him up.

Michelle Right, no more burgers, anyone.

John We wait all day for the food and when it's ready we can't have it.

Michelle I'll put more on now.

Michelle takes the unwanted burgers off the barbecue, putting them into a plastic bag. Eddie stands in the doorway, watching.

John (*to Donna*) So d'you think the curse of the dead pets is following you?

Donna Don't take the piss, Dad. Y'know it could be. I think the spirits in our street are very restless. They might be moving about, following us because we're in tune. We're receptive.

Brian Because you're fuckin' bonkers.

Michelle gets more food from the kitchen and puts it on the barbecue.

Michelle Sausages and chicken, we'll do it all together.

John This is like some sort of torture. Where you keep on being told about food but you never get any.

Donna (*looking out the doorway*) Isn't someone gonna move it? It's knocking me sick.

Brian Well, stop looking at it.

Michelle (*coming in from the barbecue*) That shouldn't take too long. Can we just forget about the cat?

Donna We've got to do something. We can't just leave it there.

John Chuck it on the barbie, I don't care what I eat now.

Brian You could make a nice pair of slippers out of that fur.

Kathleen We'll be 'ere all day.

Kathleen goes into the kitchen, gets a plastic shopping bag and heads out into the garden.

Michelle Right, shall we all go and sit down the garden?

Donna Do we have to? I don't like the garden now.

Michelle Stop it, Donna. Look, it's all set up.

Donna, John and Brian all watch Kathleen out in the garden. Michelle brings plates and cutlery out of the kitchen and places them on the table by the door.

Donna (*watching closely*) I can't look. Eeeh, look at its head all flopping about.

John It looks like it was ran over by a car, its neck looks broken.

Brian Maybe it got hit out the front and the force catapulted it over the top of Amytville and into that bush.

Michelle Don't be stupid, Brian. And will you stop calling this house Amytville.

Kathleen comes back in with the cat in the bag. The shape of it can be seen against the white plastic. She ties a knot in the handles.

Kathleen In the bin? (*She goes out to the bins at the front door.*)

Donna (*looking round the room*) What's she gonna do next?

Michelle Will you pack it in? I've got to sleep here. Come on, we're all going outside.

No one moves.

It'll be nice. I've set up candles in the trees for when it gets dark.

Robert comes through, changed and cleaned up.

Michelle Here, everyone take something. (*She passes stuff amongst them and they take it down to the garden.*) Plates. Cutlery. Ee are, Mum, will you take the salad?

Donna Oh Eddie, your tablets. (*She goes into the kitchen and pours a glass of Coke.*)

Brian Is there any more drink?

Michelle Yes, Brian. (*She passes him some wine and beer.*) There we go.

Donna (*to Michelle*) He won't drink water. (*Donna takes tablets out of her bag and gives Eddie them with the drink.*) That's better. (*going outside*) I hope there aren't any more dead animals hiding in the undergrowth.

Kathleen Oh, it's beautiful.

They all head outside. Eddie takes the tablets out of his mouth and drops them into the vase of flowers. He goes back into the television room.
Michelle moves to go.

Michelle Are you coming?

Robert In a second.

Michelle You poor thing. How's your scar? It's like you're initiated now, you're accepted.

Robert Aren't I lucky. You should have seen him, it was like something off the Jerry Springer show. I'd been having a good laugh with him but you only have to tap the surface and it all comes out.

Michelle It sounded like he did you a favour.

Robert I would have been able to deal with it. I'm not totally incompetent, you know.

Michelle I know, I know.

Robert We have made the right decision moving here, haven't we?

Michelle That could have happened anywhere. Just think of the things we've seen in London.

Robert is silent.

Oh, I can't be dealing with this now, I'm just starting to enjoy myself. Can't we talk about this later?

Robert Have you told them yet?

Michelle No, but I will, it's going to be fine, I know it is.

John (*coming back in*) You can't send us all out, then not come yourself. Come on, it's your party. (*He takes her hand.*)

Robert I'll be right down.

John and Michelle go out into the garden.
Robert goes into the kitchen and pours himself a large whisky. He comes back into the living room and takes a sip. He looks out into the garden and knocks it back in one.
Kirsty comes in from the toilet.

Kirsty Another whisky, eh?

Robert (*moving to go*) Shall we go and join the others?

Kirsty So did you sneak out in the middle of the night? Or does she know you spent the night in a lap-dancing club? Maybe she sends y' out to get y' all revved up and when y' come back she can have y' all to herself.

Robert As I said, you must be thinking of someone else. People always think they've met me when they haven't.

Kirsty D'you think I'm stupid?

Robert You mustn't say anything.

Kirsty Why not? That's my auntie there.

Robert I was only looking.

Kirsty Then what's the problem? We might as well let her know.

Robert I could tell them you work there.

Kirsty They know I've got a job. They're dead proud of me. So they don't know where I actually work. Anyway, I'm only a waitress, a barmaid, it's not like I'm taking me clothes off.

Robert You don't wear much to take off.

Kirsty I think I look good.

Robert You do.

Pause.

Kirsty I love working there. I watch the girls from behind the bar and it's like watching pop stars. They're real professionals. The blokes can't get enough. Some of them get obsessed with one of the girls and they'll be in every night. They send them cards, flowers, champagne. One bloke bought this girl a sports car. A big fuck-off . . . red one. They'll do anything to get near them. And you should see these blokes. Most of them haven't got much money. You know they're spending every last penny they've got coming. And they'll be there every night. They're sad, really.

Robert I was just walking round the streets, I needed a drink, it was the only place still open.

Kirsty Yeah.

Robert We'd had a row. I had to get out. I'd never been to anywhere like that before. I thought, nobody knows me.

Kirsty Did you recognise me as soon as I came in 'ere?

Robert Mmm, yeah.

Kirsty smiles, she's enjoying the attention.

Kirsty There was some bloke in the other night, couldn't take his eyes off me. No one normally looks at us. Why should they when there's a girl wearing just a lassy band waving her knockers in y' face. They're not interested in the moose pouring the drinks. I'd never been noticed before. I felt like one of them. I felt special. I loved it. He asked for my number but I played it dead cool . . . He was older than me grandad. I've worked out that if I bend right down when I'm serving they notice me. You noticed me.

Robert You were serving me, you were hard to miss.

Kirsty Were you waiting for me to bend down to see if I was wearing any knickers?

Robert I . . .

Kirsty That's what they're all looking for. Did you like the way me Wonderbra pushes me tits together?

No answer. He looks out to the garden to see if everyone's still at the bottom. He moves closer to Kirsty.

Kirsty You're not allowed to touch in the club. I'm sure y' know, there's signs everywhere. And that's the thing all the blokes want. They just want someone to touch. Something to feel. They hang around outside waiting for the girls like trainspotters, 'cause they know outside the club there's no rules. They can touch till their hearts' content. Have you still got mates living in London?

Robert (*moving closer to her*) Yeah.

Kirsty What I was thinking is, I could stay with them . . .

> *Robert moves in close, almost touching. He moves to kiss her. Michelle walks in with some empty beer bottles in her hand. She stops and sees Robert and Kirsty, she heads back outside quickly.*
> *Robert tries to kiss Kirsty and put a hand on her breast. It's messy and awkward. Kirsty is unnerved, she doesn't know how to handle this. She tries to push him away.*

Kirsty What d'you think you're doing?

Robert What you want me to do.

Kirsty Who d'you think I am?

Robert Oh yeah, you know what you're doing.

> *He leans forward and kisses her again. She pushes him away.*

Kirsty D'you think I'm always up for it, like you? I don't want it.

Robert You do.

> *He goes to kiss her again, she moves away.*

Kirsty Get away from me, you creep. You're just like all the pervs in the club.

Robert Come on, what was that all about?

Kirsty All what? I was just talking to y'.

Brian (*coming in*) Are you going in or what?

Brian comes in, followed by Michelle.

Brian She says she's going to get more drink and she's just standing outside the door staring at the sky. What's wrong with y'?

Michelle I was looking at the sunset.

Michelle looks at Robert, he moves as far away as possible from Kirsty.

Brian I'm just . . . (*Brian goes off to the toilet.*)

Robert (*moving towards the garden*) How is it down there? We should all . . .

Kirsty I've gotta go. I've got to meet me mates and I'm in work later. I'll leave you to it. (*She walks to the french windows.*) Mum, I'm off. Will Reinar be all right with you? (*She doesn't wait for an answer.*) See ya. (*She walks to the door to the hall and stops. To Robert*) Might see you down the lap-dancing club again tonight, eh? See ya. (*She takes out her phone, dials a number and leaves.*) . . . Hiya, it's me. I'm on me way.

Pause. An awkward silence as Michelle and Robert are left alone.

Michelle Oh, so how was the lap-dancing club? Why didn't you tell us earlier that you'd already been?

Robert It was just one of those stupid things I ended up doing . . .

Michelle One of many.

Robert Here we go.

Michelle Bored of me already? Is that why you walked out last night?

Robert I walked out because I couldn't bear to listen to all this.

Michelle What I would like to know is why you were trying to shove your tongue down my niece's throat?

Pause. Robert is speechless. Brian comes back in, sniffing, smoking and very talkative.

Brian This house is boss. I could really get used to it here. Haven't you made it back down with that booze yet? I suppose I'd better get it meself. (*He goes into the kitchen.*) I'll take some beer and some vodka, it's a long walk down there. (*He comes back out with his arms full.*) We're going to drink this house dry. (*He goes back outside.*)

Robert I can explain.

Michelle I don't know whether I'm interested, you know.

Robert It's been a weird day. I'm all over the place. I don't know anyone.

Michelle I'm just embarrassed. Embarrassed for you. Throwing yourself at her. Thinking that she would fancy you.

Robert We can sort this out.

Michelle Are you always going to fuck up?

Robert I'm glad you have so much faith in me.

Michelle Well, stop giving me the ammunition. Give me something to have faith in, believe in.

Robert If you'd give me the chance . . .

Michelle You're not interested in me.

Robert Do we have to go through this all again. I'm here, aren't I?

Michelle You're only here because you can coast along a bit longer and not decide what to do with your life.

Robert Like being with you is easy.

Michelle Just seeing you next to my family. Maybe you're what I was trying to get away from.

Robert You don't fit in here.

Michelle I do.

Robert You're different people, you've changed. That's if you ever had anything in common in the first place.

Michelle No, they understand me.

Robert You can't even tell them what job you're doing.

Michelle I will. They know me better than anyone else and I know they'll understand. They understand me and you don't.

Robert moves to go.

Robert I've had enough of this.

Michelle Go on, walk out, that's your answer to everything.

Robert I'd love to stay around to see the great moment when they understand you. I'd like to see that. They're the last people who understand you. You're right, I don't understand you.

Michelle Stay or go I don't care. I'm sure the lap-dancing club will be opening soon, why don't you go there?

Robert At least I'll get some stimulation there.

Robert walks out, down the hall and out the front door, slamming the door behind him.
Michelle stands proud in the middle of the living room. She breathes deeply. She crumbles, on the verge

*of tears. She tries to compose herself. Eddie appears in
the hall door behind her. She becomes aware of
someone standing behind her and turns quickly. She
sees him and jumps slightly.*

Michelle Did you hear all that?

Eddie just looks at her.

Of course you did. Do you want to go outside with
everyone else?

Eddie doesn't move.

Suit yourself.

*Michelle picks up a glass from the table by the door
and goes into the kitchen to make herself a stiff drink.
Eddie wanders round the room. He looks at the
remnants of the game on the coffee table. He sits on
top of the table and sees that it's on wheels. He rocks
it back and forth, playing about. He reveals the black
soot mark and, intrigued, moves the table to see the
rest of the stain. Michelle comes in from the kitchen
with a drink. She sees the mark on the rug.*

Michelle Have you just done that? What have you done?
That's a brand new rug.

Eddie looks at her.

You're not at home now, you can play these games with
your mum but I'm not having this going on in my house.
You little . . .

Eddie steps back, a bit frightened.

Oh, I'm so sorry, Eddie, what am I thinking? What am
I doing? (*She kneels down in front of him so she's on a
level with him and takes his hands.*) I'm sorry, I didn't
mean to shout. I'm just . . . Come here.

She wraps her arms round him and gives him a big hug, he stands stiff with his arms by his sides. She holds him tight. He slowly lifts his arms and hugs her back, gentle at first and then tight like he's never done it before.

That's it.

They hold each other. Michelle breaks it, she holds his arms.

Thank you. That's just what I needed.

She looks at him. Eddie looks around and then slowly opens his mouth to speak. Donna comes in.

Donna (*coming in*) I like the way Brian just gets drinks for him. What are y' hiding up here for?

Eddie moves away quickly from Michelle. Donna heads to the kitchen. She sees the stained rug.

Donna What's happened there?

Michelle Nothing, we just had a little accident.

Donna That on the rug? You did it?

Michelle No . . .

Donna Oh, Eddie did it? Did you see him do it?

Michelle Well, no . . . but . . . he probably . . .

Donna (*to Eddie*) Did you do that?

Eddie shakes his head.

(*to Eddie*) Go outside.

Eddie goes out into the garden.

It's this fuckin' house, it's not him.

Michelle Oh yeah, it was the ghost of Mrs Winstanley again.

Donna It could have been anyone. You sound like Brian. Just because Eddie's there doesn't mean it was him.

Michelle Of course he did. This is what he does. If you want to find out where the poltergeist is, look no further.

Donna What are you saying about my son?

Michelle I think he needs help.

Donna How would you know anything about children? You wouldn't even know how to look after a fuckin' yucca plant.

Michelle Listen . . .

Donna Naah, I don't want to listen . . .

Kathleen (*coming in*) Donna. Michelle. Oh look at that on your nice new rug.

Donna She reckons our Eddie did it.

Michelle I just . . .

Kathleen Eddie wouldn't do that. Now you wanna get something on that quick, or you'll never get it off. Fairy Liquid. Where's y' Fairy Liquid? Gets rid of soot a treat.

Kathleen goes into the kitchen.

Michelle Mum.

Michelle and Donna are left alone.

I'm . . . (*sorry*).

Donna Forget it. You're a fuckin' nightmare sometimes, y'know.

Kathleen comes in with a bucket, washing-up liquid and a cloth. Donna goes into the kitchen. Kathleen starts cleaning the rug.

Michelle Mum, leave it.

Kathleen I couldn't. You don't wanna be staring at this stain for the rest of y' life.

Kathleen starts to clean the stain. Michelle watches.

I'll just put this on, give it a scrub and leave it for a while. It should draw it all out. I wonder how it happened? Maybe a hot coal spat off the barbecue and jumped across the room.

Michelle Maybe.

Kathleen This reminds me of when I cleaned for Mrs Heathcote. Her house was just like this one, only she had all those dogs. Dog hairs everywhere.

Michelle Don't you clean for her any more?

Kathleen Oh no, I haven't for ages. Not since y' dad got finished up. I couldn't go out to work while he was sitting at home, it'd be rubbing his face in it. I'm not saying we couldn't have done with the money but it would have been more trouble than it was worth. I did miss it, though, it was me little escape a couple of times a week. Now I just go to mass instead. I don't know what I'd do without it. I used to pretend that it was my house, think that I was lady of the manor. (*the rug*) It's quite ingrained.

Michelle You know this job me dad's talking about? Well . . .

Kathleen Y' see, in a way it's all worked itself out, hasn't it? Me prayers have paid off. He's got that job and . . . maybe I could go back, I could give her a call. I think she's still alive.

Michelle But what if there isn't a job at Cammell Lairds?

Kathleen There is, you heard him. There's some new firm taking it over.

Pause. Michelle walks over to the doors and looks out into the garden.

Kathleen Where's Robert got to?

Michelle He's gone out, for a walk.

Kathleen He should be resting, not walking round.

Pause.

Michelle You know I was saying about my new job?

Kathleen At Cadbury's. Oh, are you going to tell us what you're making?

Michelle No, no. I'm not working at Cadbury's.

Kathleen You're not.

Michelle It was a joke. That didn't really work, wasn't funny. I wanted to tell you earlier, but, me dad needs to know. I'm working at Cammell Lairds, what was Cammell Lairds.

Kathleen (*she stops cleaning*) Y' what?

Michelle I'm part of the new management team that's taking over the site.

Donna appears in the hall doorway with an open bottle of wine. She listens.

Kathleen God, who'd have thought, you and Cammell Lairds. But then I've never understood what your job is. Oh, well done, that's great that is, Michelle.

Michelle sees Donna.

Donna Did I hear right?

Michelle Well . . . yeah.

Kathleen Isn't it great?

Donna I suppose so. It's just bizarre. You working in a place where they build ships, where it's dirty and they've got oil. You couldn't wear that there.

Kathleen Oh, stop it, Donna.

Donna And the Cadbury's song and dance?

Kathleen It was a joke.

Donna That was a joke?

Michelle I didn't know what else to say.

Kathleen Oh, you must tell y' dad. He'd be so proud.

Donna looks at Michelle, she can see she's uncomfortable.

He'll definitely have the job now, you'll be able to sort him out. Oh, I'm so pleased for the both of y'.

Michelle But it's going to be different . . .

Kathleen I'm sure it is. (*the rug*) That should do the trick. Now you've got to leave it for a while and then we'll give it another good scrub.

Michelle No . . . .

Kathleen (*taking the bucket and liquid back into the kitchen*) Oh, you have to, or it'll never come out.

Donna can see how exasperated Michelle is.

Donna What's going on?

Kathleen (*coming back out*) I'll finish it off, then I could come round in the morning and have a look at it.

Michelle I need to explain, Mum . . .

Kathleen I'll go and get y' dad.

Michelle No.

Kathleen You've gotta tell him, Michelle, he'd be over the moon.

Michelle No, Mother, I don't want you to tell him.

Donna Oi, wind your neck in, you.

Kathleen I suppose you want to tell him yourself. I won't say a word, my lips are sealed.

Kathleen goes into the garden. Michelle and Donna are left alone.

Donna Will you stop biting her head off?

Pause.

Michelle Why doesn't she listen? She's got it all wrong.

Donna So you are working at Cadbury's, then?

Michelle I'm involved with the redevelopment of Cammell Lairds. The site. I'm not doing anything to do with ships, I don't know the first thing. Cammell Lairds as a shipbuilder is over. It went into receivership and it's not coming out again. I know it's closed before, but this time it's for good.

Donna So what about me dad's job?

Michelle There isn't a job.

Donna What about this new firm, the new ships me dad was talking about?

Michelle There aren't any new ships. It's over. I don't know where he got it from.

Donna So you've come back here to close it down?

Michelle No, I've got nothing to do with it closing down. That's already happened. It's been on its last legs for years. Struggling from one crisis to the next.

Donna But you're sealing its fate, putting a full stop on it. There'll be no chance of shipbuilding coming back once you've 'redeveloped' it.

Michelle I think it's a good thing that it's over. A town can't rely on one industry any more. We can start afresh and make something new of it. Shipbuilding's over. We don't need big massive ships any more, and if we do, someone in Korea will make them for a quarter of what we could. Yeah, it employed most of the people in this town at one point. It made this town. Even this house was built on the back of it. But it's over now and we've got to move on to the future.

Donna This is what you've come back for?

Michelle I'm only part of the team looking at the options, but I'm proud to be involved with it. Isn't it better to make the most of the land rather than just let it go to waste?

Donna So what are we getting in its place, another shopping centre?

Michelle There will be shops, but other things as well, it's a big site. I'm mainly involved with the housing, but there'll be new businesses, a bit of tourism, maybe a sports arena. It's very early days. I think it's going to be really exciting. You know, there'll be a lot of money going into it. We already know we can get huge grants off Europe and the government. They're throwing money at things like this.

Donna Oh, I know what it's gonna be. It'll be all posh warehouse flats and poncey shops, poncey bars and poncey restaurants.

Michelle It won't be like that.

Donna And how about a museum showing what used to be made there. But only a small one because we don't want to dwell on the past too much.

Michelle I think it's important to keep the history of the place still alive in whatever happens. I'm fighting to keep it called Cammell Lairds rather than some meaningless made-up name like River Village. And I think we should involve the men who used to build the ships in whatever happens.

Donna Well you've got someone who'll look after the car park out in your garden.

Michelle Oh, Donna.

Donna I tell you what you must have. A marina, that's just what Birkenhead needs, so all the snobs from Cheshire can keep their boats there. And we'll get a nice bypass built so they can avoid seeing the people who actually live here when they're on their way to pick up their yacht. Oh, it'll be lovely. That's just what this town needs. So people can feel more fuckin' alienated.

Michelle You're just being ridiculous.

Donna No, I'm not. Just look at Liverpool. Bars and flats in the city centre all for the same people. One square mile of wealth doesn't do anything for the surrounding twenty miles. All the same poncey people live there, eat there, shop there, and the money doesn't touch the people who really need it, who live down the road. They build big fences and big gates or just make it so intimidating that we know we're not allowed.

Michelle Would you rather have it that there's nothing new happening, that the whole town is crumbling down, everyone moving away?

Donna Are we meant to be grateful for you moving back?

Michelle No, but I'm trying to do some good. Whatever's built there will have the same impact Cammell Lairds has had. It could completely change what this town's all about, put it back on the map.

Donna Yeah, turn it into a theme park for tourists.

Michelle We're going to consult the local people and ask them what they want.

Donna I can tell you now, they want proper jobs not crappy part-time ones stuck behind a till or answering phones.

Michelle I know it means big changes. But we've got to look to the future. It's all service industries now, that's where the jobs are. The days of a job for life are over. People have got to learn to adapt, to be flexible.

Donna Adapt? Flexible? It just means they can treat you like shit, send you home if it's quiet and you don't know if you've got a job one week to the next.

Michelle You're living in some nostalgic fantasy land where everything was lovely when we were kids. Everyone loved their jobs and had happy home lives sat round the fire. Was it really like that? Was it really that good?

Donna I know things weren't perfect, but look at it now.

Michelle Come on, Donna, the men building ships were working in cramped, dirty, unhealthy conditions. Working long hours, they never saw their families. It wasn't nice.

And for women it was really oppressive, they had no choices.

Donna And they've got everything to choose from now?

Michelle We don't live in an ideal world, Donna.

Donna If anyone thought we did, it was you.

Michelle We've got to work with the reality of the situation, the real world, and things are getting better.

Donna What do you know about reality? What sort of reality do you live in? Eh? Where all you've got to worry about is the street being too crowded and you're late for a meeting. Or the Tube being a bit smelly. This is reality. My family is reality. A psycho child who's got me wrapped round his little finger. A lazy depressed fella and a daughter who thinks she's Britney fuckin' Spears. My reality is working nights and split shifts packing fuckin' peanuts. Paying one loan off with another, buying everything off the catalogue in fifty-two weekly instalments. The reality of having to borrow two quid off your mum till the end of the week. Trying to keep it all together. And it's all down to me, no one else. If I stop for one minute, it all falls apart.

Michelle I know it's hard, I understand, this is where I'm from . . .

Donna Yeah, and a lots changed since you lived 'ere, it's getting worse and we don't need people like you coming back 'ere telling us how to live.

Michelle Donna, you've got it wrong.

Donna But you know what we've got, we've got the best thing anyone could want. We've got friendly people . . .

Michelle Oh Donna, I didn't mean it like . . .

Donna Why would we need good jobs or a future because the bloke on the bus says thank you when you get off and people hold the door open for y' in Asda? Life just can't get any better for me.

Michelle You know it's more than that.

Donna Why did you come back, eh? To rub our faces in it? To fuck us up the arse?

Michelle It was only a matter of time before you started screaming at me.

Donna It's the only way I'll get a word in or get you to listen.

Michelle You get off on this, you'd rather have it that the whole world's against you than do anything. Nothing's gonna change round here if people still won't listen to anyone from outside.

Donna Oh, I didn't realise you've come back to help us, to save us from ourselves. Don't worry, it won't last long. You'll get bored when you realise you can't control everyone and it's not the romanticised little dream world you'd remembered it as.

Michelle You've always had a chip on your shoulder, ever since I left home. You could have moved away, you were just too scared.

Donna I could do. I dream about just walking out, leaving them. Being free. Starting again somewhere else, but I can't just run away.

Michelle It's not running, it's about deciding what you want and taking a risk. It's like moving back here, it's a risk but I'm going to make it work.

Donna You've only come back here because it hasn't worked in London. You got sacked from your last job and your relationship's on the bones of its arse. When you were all successful and Mrs Career you didn't want to know us, but now it's all going pear-shaped you need us again. And you can come back 'ere and look like a success because you've got a big house.

Michelle It's not like that, it isn't.

Donna Isn't it?

Michelle No, no, it's more than that. I want to do something. (*She starts to become upset.*) To make a difference, be part of something.

Donna Don't start booing again.

Michelle This is where I belong. It has to be, I've got nothing else. You're all I've got. This is the only place where I feel I get near to who I am.

Donna You've got everything. You can do whatever you want.

Michelle A career, money, a house with five bedrooms. Who needs five bedrooms? What does it matter if you're on your own? If you feel like you don't fit in anywhere, you don't belong anywhere. I've been so busy being ambitious and always moving on, looking for something else. Recreating myself. I don't know who I am any more. What I want. I thought the answer was children. Have children and I can stop worrying about myself. I can feel like I've done something worthwhile, but I can't even do that.

Donna You and Robert will sort yourselves out.

Michelle Oh, come on, we're dead in the water. We have been for ages. He does me head in. This book crap. He's never going to write a book. It'll be something else next year. And he always knows that if it gets a bit tight he can call one of Daddy's friends and they'll give him a job just like that.

Donna You'll work it out.

Michelle I can't remember the last time we slept together. He even tried to get off with Kirsty.

Donna He didn't? (*She smiles.*) Oh, I know it's not funny, but . . .

Michelle I have to make this work. I don't know what to do if this doesn't work.

Donna It will, it will.

Michelle I need you. I don't belong with someone like him, I never did. You and me mum and dad are all I've got. I don't know what I'd do if I didn't have you.

Donna Oh stop it, you're gonna make me throw up.

Michelle smiles.

Michelle God, I always wanted to be more like you. The funny one who gets on with everyone. I was always the nervous one in the background pissing people off.

Donna And here's me wishing I'd done half the things that you've done.

They look at each other and smile, a moment between them. Pause.
John, Kathleen and Brian come in.

Kathleen I couldn't help it. I had to tell him.

Michelle looks to Donna.

John What's this all about? Are we ever going to get any food?

Brian Is this another one of your games, 'Chelle?

Michelle doesn't answer.

Kathleen Go on, tell him what you told me.

John You're not working at Cammell Lairds, are you?

Pause.

Michelle No, I'm not.

Kathleen Yes, you are. I don't understand.

Michelle No, Mother, you've got it wrong.

They all look to Michelle.

John Spit it out, what is it then?

Donna Shall we leave this for now? Let's have some food.

John Come on, I'd like to know what's going on.

Kathleen So would I.

Pause.

Michelle I am going to be working at what was Cammell Lairds, but turning it into something else.

Kathleen See, I told you it was great.

Donna Will you shut up for a minute, Mother. It's not great.

John Don't speak to y' mother like that. (*to Michelle*) You're what?

Michelle My job is to work on the redevelopment of the site. To build houses, new businesses on it. There isn't going to be any more shipbuilding.

John is silent.

It's nothing to do with me, I'm just here to try and make something of it. I didn't know anything about these rumours. If I could change it back, Dad, I would. I'd do anything.

Kathleen But . . . your dad's been told he's got a job, haven't y'?

No answer.

Haven't y'?

Donna Leave it, Mum.

Kathleen But if y' dad's been told, then they can't do this. There must be something you can do. They've got to give you your job back. They've got to. (*Pause.*) John?

John I knew there was no jobs. Deep down, I knew nothing would come of it. You can go a long way on false hope. I haven't really believed in anything for years.

Kathleen But what about the other men, weren't they told?

John No love, just like me. We all sat round in the pub and through a few rumours we convinced ourselves. We had to.

Kathleen (*becoming teary*) I can't go through this again.

Michelle There'll be other jobs, new jobs in this new development. I can guarantee that.

John Not for me, there won't.

Michelle There will, Dad.

Pause.

John We should go.

Michelle No, no, don't. You can't go.

Kathleen Yeah, come on.

Michelle The food'll be ready now.

John I'm not hungry.

Michelle Please stay. You can't go, leaving it like this.

Kathleen Robert'll be back soon. Are you coming Donna?

Michelle looks to Donna. Pause.

Donna (*quiet*) Yeah.

Eddie stands at the door. Donna waves him over to her.

Brian I'll see ya, 'Chelle.

Donna Yeah, 'bye.

Michelle (*to Donna*) Are you sure?

Donna Yeah, I think it's best.

Donna, Brian and Eddie make their way out.

Kathleen Ta ra, Michelle.

John Bye.

John goes up and gives her a kiss and a hug, she holds him tightly. He breaks away.

Michelle I wanted you to be proud of me.

Pause.

If it's money, I can help you out. I can give you . . .

John That's the last thing it is. 'Bye, Michelle.

John and Kathleen leave.
Michelle is left alone. She stands in the middle of the room. She breathes heavily, tears flow down her cheeks. She looks around the room not knowing what

*to do. She sees the barbecue. She picks up a plate and
starts taking the food off it. Reinar starts to cry from
upstairs. Michelle stops and listens. She puts the plate
down and goes upstairs. Reinar continues to cry. He
stops for a second and then cries some more. Michelle
comes down the stairs and into the living room
carrying Reinar. A real tiny baby. She sits down on
the sofa with him and rocks him.*

Michelle Everything's going to be all right. Shush. I'll
look after you now.

He stops crying.